Wallace W Nixon

The Chemical Laundry Guide

a work designed to teach ladies the art of laundrying clothes according to chemical principals and the superior methods employed by city laundries, containing a full and explicit treatise on linen polishing

Wallace W Nixon

The Chemical Laundry Guide
a work designed to teach ladies the art of laundrying clothes according to chemical principals and the superior methods employed by city laundries, containing a full and explicit treatise on linen polishing

ISBN/EAN: 9783337291686

Printed in Europe, USA, Canada, Australia, Japan

Cover: Foto ©Andreas Hilbeck / pixelio.de

More available books at **www.hansebooks.com**

THE CHEMICAL
LAUNDRY GUIDE

———A WORK———

DESIGNED TO TEACH LADIES THE ART OF LAUNDRYING CLOTHES ACCORDING TO CHEMICAL PRINCIPALS AND THE SUPERIOR METHODS EMPLOYED BY

CITY LAUNDRIES;

——— CONTAINING ———

A FULL AND EXPLICIT TREATISE

——— ON ———

LINEN POLISHING,

AND THE SKILLFUL WASHING AND RENOVATION OF ARTICLES OF EVERY MATERIAL

OVER THREE HUNDRED LAUNDRY METHODS.

WALLACE W. NIXON.

LYNCHBURG, VA.
J. P. BELL & CO.,
1879.

The Combined Corrugated Glossing and Molding Iron.

FAMILY RIGHT,

This is to Certify, that I have this day sold to

_____

the right to use, repair, make, or cause to be repaired or made, for ___ use, **Wallace W. Nixon's Patent Self-Adjusting Shirt Board, Combined Corrugated Glossing and Molding Iron, and Copyrighted Chemical Laundry Guide**, the same to be used in no other place or places.

This _____ 18____   _____ Agent.

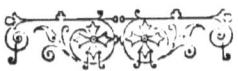

2.—PURCHASING CONTRACT.

THE Self-Adjusting Shirt Board, the Combined Corrugated Glossing and Molding Iron, are each secured by United States Letters Patent, (No. 206,350 and No. 210,551, granted, July 23rd, '78 and Dec. 3rd, '78, respectively;) and the Chemical Laundry Guide is secured by Copyright. These articles cannot be purchased from any firm or stores, nor are they *Sold* under any circumstances; they are merely given away to purchasers of Family Rights. It is only the Family Right that is sold, and for the use of the purchasers only. Any person or persons found using or manufacturing any of these Patents without a legitimate right, will be fully prosecuted. It is a part of the consideration of the purchasing contract, and is agreed to by the purchaser of the Family Right, not to lend the articles.

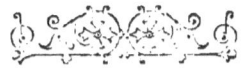

3.—PREFACE.

THE Chemical Laundry Guide is submitted to the public to supply a want that has long existed, for a reliable laundry guide for family use. Gentlemen who have ever had their linen done up at a fashionable city laundry, are delighted with the beautiful gloss and pearl finish that is given it. They also admire its clearness and stiffness, and notice how much longer their linen done up in that style, keeps clean. They wonder why it cannot be done with the same skill at home. Ladies who send various articles, lace curtains, dresses, linen suits, laces, etc., to the city laundry, receive them back looking as bright and having the same lustre as when bought at the store new. They admire and wonder how it is done, but the methods employed are to them profound secrets. There is no magic about them, however. The methods are simple and easy to follow. If ladies only understood them, they could have the pleasure and satisfaction of doing up articles at home in the laundry style. Every lady knows how to wash and iron in the usual way; but at a large laundry establishment, where the most experienced and skilled help, (even the celebrated French laundress from Paris,) is employed, where laundry work is in process every week-day of the year, where large sums of money are expended in making experiments, it is no wonder that such an establishment should possess methods vastly superior to those employed by the family, or washerwoman.

Laundry work is now a profession, as is evinced by the perfection of work attained by the laundries of the East. It is the design of the Chemical Laundry Guide, to teach ladies how to do up articles in a style equal to that of the best French laundress.

The author has had extensive experience in laundry work, having himself worked in one of the best laundries the country affords, and having been engaged for several years in teaching fine laundry work in large cities. He has also visited a number of noted laundries, and investigated and studied their methods.

A book of this kind, however, in order to be complete and contain reliable methods embracing every department of scientific laundry work, and fully treating of the successful renovation of articles of every material, must of necessity, partake of the nature of a compiled work. The major part of the methods and directions presented, are those now employed by the best laundries, and the author learned them directly from the laundries.

He is also indebted to Muspratt's Chemistry applied to the arts, Dick's Encyclopedia, Goodholmes Encyclopedia, Inquire Within, and other sources too numerous to admit of acknowledgement. Also many new and useful laundry methods and expedients have been met, and a practical knowledge of their merits gained, during several years of travel in teaching the very work itself. From such varied and extensive opportunities, the author has gleaned much valuable information respecting laundry work, which could in no other way be obtained. No method or direction is presented but what has been thoroughly tested, and is eminently practical and reliable. It has been the aim, not only to make the directions full and explicit, but also to give the theories upon which the methods are based, and to so explain the principles upon which the various reagents act, that the knowledge of each method may be thorough and complete.

NORTH GARDEN, VA.,   W. W. NIXON.

June, 1879.

4.—CONTENTS.

PART I.

CHAPTER. PAGE.
I. Glossing Linen.................................... 15
II. Various Starches and their Use.............. 36
III. Washing... 51
IV. Soaps of Domestic Manufacture............. 64
V. Stains on Linen and Cotton.................. 81
VI. Care of Linen..................................... 103
VII. Improved Method of Cutting and Making Shirts... 111

PART II.

VIII. Printed Goods of Delicate Colors...........140
IX. Woolens and Flannels..........................151
X. Renovation of Silks.............................164
XI. Laces, Satins, Velvets, &c....................186
XII. Gentlemen's Clothing..........................212
XIII. Renovation of Carpets.........................226
XIV. Renovation of Beds and Bedding...........240
General Index from..................253 to 274

5.—INTRODUCTION.

AT the outset, an explanation of the purpose and scope of the Chemical Laundry Guide, may be of benefit to the beginner in the art of fine laundry work.

Every lady is in practical posession of the elements of washing and ironing, and this work is intended to supplement this practical knowledge, by presenting methods that will afford easier and happier results, make the finesse of fine laundry work familiar, and awaken a definite interest in this most essential domestic art. Ladies are by far too conservative. They steadfastly follow old methods, leaving to the specialist in domestic arts, to discover and profit by superior methods, and to accomplish what they never imagined could be done. No doubt agents, when introducing this subject, will be often met with the assertion, that ladies already know too much about washing and ironing. Forsooth, there is too intimate an acquaintance with the ways our foremothers did household work, but in this progressive age domestic arts have made wonderful advancement, as well as general science and the polite arts, and there is much that can be learned even by the oldest and best housekeeper. The interest and satisfaction too, afforded by methods that effect quick, easy and admirable results, will turn the irksome tasks of the laundry into pleasures.

Although strictly a reference book for family use, the Chemical Laundry Guide embraces nearly every method that would be of service to the professional launderer or laundress; and its careful perusal and study will be very profitable, for many hints will be received thereby, which will suggest experiments never before thought of in this branch of domestic economy. Whenever choice and delicate articles of any material require laundrying or renovating, the Chemical Laundry Guide may be profitably consulted. The index at the end of the book will be found especially convenient for reference. By reading the Explanation of the Index, (317) its plan and arrangement will be readily understood. The methods are numbered, and wherever numerals occur in the context, they refer to the methods of those numbers and not to the page numbers: and to avoid needless repetition, where other methods have an important bearing upon the one under consideration, references are given. It is always advisable to look up the references.

Many ladies may think perhaps, that the directions in these methods are too precise and over nice, that it makes little difference, whether soft or hard water, white or yellow soap, one or two washing and rinsing waters be used. The fact, however, cannot be too strongly urged that the more exactness with which nice laundry operations are conducted, the more perfect and pleasing will be the result. This idea of exactness is recognized in every other science, and why should it not be likewise in this? If the directions be closely followed, even the most variable methods will rarely fail.

In several of the departments, and especially in the removal of various stains, two or more methods are presented for nearly the same purpose, and a lady may be puzzled in respect to which it is best to employ. Natural judgement, however, will seldom lead astray. Every method presented is essential to some form of laundry work, some case, or some material. It not unfrequently happens, however, in the more variable phases of laundry work, that one method will produce the desired effect in one case, and a happy result will follow, while the same method and precisely the same treatment for what is considered a similar case, will have little or no effect; hence it is necessary to resort to some other treatment, to suit the particular case under experiment. To meet all cases, therefore, have the several different methods been introduced. And when any particular one has been selected for any particular case, and it does not have the desired effect, it will only be necessary to resort to another, being careful always not to condemn the first treatment, until it has been thoroughly tested. Such perplexity is not likely to occur, unless it be with very obdurate cases.

The various chemicals employed in the methods, will not injure the finest fabric nor the most delicate of colors, if used according to directions. Full directions accompany their use, and where precaution is required, it is stated. No lady, therefore, need hesitate to employ any method, because the chemical agent is not familiar. The cost of nearly all these chemicals are trifling, and they may be obtained of any druggist.

CHAPTER I.

6.—GLOSSING LINEN.

THE art of polishing linen or giving starched articles the same gloss and pearl finish they posess when first purchased, is little understood outside of regular laundries. It may be easily acquired, however, and its benefits are manifold. One of its chief advantages is, the great length of time that glossed articles will keep clean. Dirt cannot grime into the fabric, but slides off the glassy surface. Everyone is aware, how long new collars and cuffs will wear without soiling,--twice as long as the home done up collar. Again, the stiffness is retained by the gloss. Ladies often notice that when articles starched in the usual manner, are laid away, they soon become limp and the stiffness departs. It seems as though the starch evaporates. Especially is this the case in wet weather. Glossed articles, on the contrary, retain their stiffness in defiance of moisture, for any length of time. Ample proof of this is afforded by new shirts; may be they lay in stores for years, before they are sold, yet they are always firm and stiff. This characteristic of the gloss particularly adapts it for the edges of fine curtains and choice pillow slips, where it is desirable that such articles should keep clean and stiff for a long time. Another excellent point is, that when polished articles become soiled, they can be washed so readily. The dirt has not penetrated into the linen, it is only on the surface; merely warm water will dissolve the enamel and remove the dirt with it. The gloss is like a varnish to protect the linen. What brings the gloss so much in demand, however. is the beautiful appearance it bestows upon linen. Even to muslins it imparts a linen finish, difficult to distinguish from the genuine linen. The remark is often passed, that a gentleman may be ever so well dressed, yet his toilet is incomplete, without the neatly done up shirt, cuffs, and collar.

Nearly everyone has supposed that polishing was done by preparing the starch some peculiar way or by putting some ingredient in it. This is not the case however. It is done entirely with the iron. Any starched article, calico and muslin, as well as linen, may be taken direct from the drawer already done up, and a beautiful gloss given it simply by the use of the glossing iron. Shirts are glossed on the same principal that boots are blacked. A boot is first dampened with blacking, then the friction of the brush develops the polish; after a shirt is ironed, it is slightly moistened with water, and the friction and heat of the glossing iron brings out the gloss. No matter from what substance, or in what manner the starch be prepared, provided only, the article contains starch as a body to work upon, a gloss may always be imparted. It is obvious, though, that an article nicely starched and very stiff, will take a better gloss than a flimsy one. No two ladies, although they may use the same quality of starch and apparently prepare it in the same manner, will produce like results; the starch of the one will be pliable, iron smoothly, and have a proper stiffness; while that of the other, will roll, stick to the iron, and be limpsy. In starch making, a great deal depends upon attention to the minutiæ and details. Below is given the laundry way of preparing starch, and the mode of applying it to the fabric. It is the most natural and simple way it can be prepared, and will doubtless appear very familiar to many ladies, as just the way they have always done; but we advise them to give careful attention to the minutiæ and details of this method, with the assurance that they will be agreeably suprised at the result. For glossing, articles should be well washed, as the dirt is more apt to be visible than on a plain surface.

The objection is often offered against polishing, that it wears and destroys the fabric. Such an objection plainly shows that those who express it are entirely ignorant of the subject. As no chemical is used to produce the gloss, how can it possibly injure the fabric, any more than common ironing? The truth is, articles that are always glossed will last much longer than when ironed in the usual way; for the obvious reason, they do not soil so easily, and the dirt can be extracted without rubbing the article to pieces.

7.—LAUNDRY METHOD OF PREPARING STARCH.

THE proportions given may be varied to suit the number of articles to be starched. Take one ounce of good bought Starch, and add just enough clear soft water to convert it into a thick paste. Knead it well between clean fingers, carefully breaking up every lump and particle. Rub it perfectly smooth, so that it may be entirely free from lumps and of the same consistency throughout. When this has been done, add to the paste nearly or quite a pint of boiling water. It should then be boiled very thoroughly at least half an hour, or even longer. It will iron more smoothly, and the full stiffening properties of the starch are better obtained by long boiling. Stir it frequently while boiling, to keep it from burning, and add a few drops of Blueing to give it a clear cast. When not stirring, cover from the dust; cover, also, when removed from the fire, to prevent a scum from rising. It is not necessary to put any ingredient in the starch, unless it be a small quantity of the purest Hog's Lard. For the above proportions of Starch and water, a lump of Lard about the size of a thimble is sufficient. The Lard prevents any rolling or sticking of the starch, and makes it iron smoothly. The starch should always be strained through muslin or a coarse towel.

8.—APPLYING THE STARCH.

IN starching shirts, it is the laundry custom to dry them previous to applying the starch. It is thought the shirts are stiffer by this means. After drying, dip the bosom and cuffs into the starch while hot as the hand can bear; then spread the shirt out smoothly upon a table or any hard surface, and, with the hands, work the adhering starch thoroughly into both sides of the linen, at the same time smoothing out the wrinkles. In this way the cloth will take up more of the starch, and the more starch the linen absorbs, of course, the stiffer it will be. By this after rubbing and smoothing out of the wrinkles, blistering also will be avoided.

9.—STARCHING COLLARS AND CUFFS.

IN laundries, collars and cuffs are usually given a second starching. After starching and rubbing in the starch the same as for shirts,(8.) they are made to dry quickly, and are then in the same manner, given a second starching, and again allowed to dry. They are not sprinkled in the usual way, but while dry, are rolled up in a wet cloth or blanket, and allowed to remain until the moisture penetrates evenly through them. It is a kind of sweating process, like the cigar maker sweats leaf tobacco. Treated in this manner, they will iron smoothly, be exceedingly stiff, and can readily be given the enamel-like finish, that always distinguishes the work of a first class laundry. The advantages will more than compensate for the extra labor, as they will keep clean and stiff twice as long as indifferently done up collars and cuffs. It is unnecessary to give shirts a second starching, unless it be desired to have them particularly stiff.

10.—SELF-ADJUSTING SHIRT BOARD.

THIS patent Shirt Board aids a lady vastly in doing up a shirt neatly, and with ease. It fits a shirt perfectly about the shoulders and neck, and stretches the wrinkles out of the plaits. Many shirts are exceedingly difficult to iron without leaving bad wrinkles; the inner lining having shrunk more than the outside linen, the edges of the shirt front will be badly wrinkled, in spite of every exertion. The Self-Adjusting Shirt Board, however, entirely overcomes this difficulty. The damp shirt front, stretched over the board, looks almost ironed; the iron is merely passed over it to dry out the moisture. The convex neck piece, at the head of the board, causes the shirt band to stand out in proper shape, and thereby, the collar will have a better fit around the neck of the wearer. The shirt bosom can also be smoothed clear up to the band. By the use of this board, a lady can iron two shirts, while she is ironing one in the usual way, and is saved the worry of pulling and stretching out the wrinkles with the hands. The Self-Adjusting Shirt Board makes shirt ironing a pleasure.

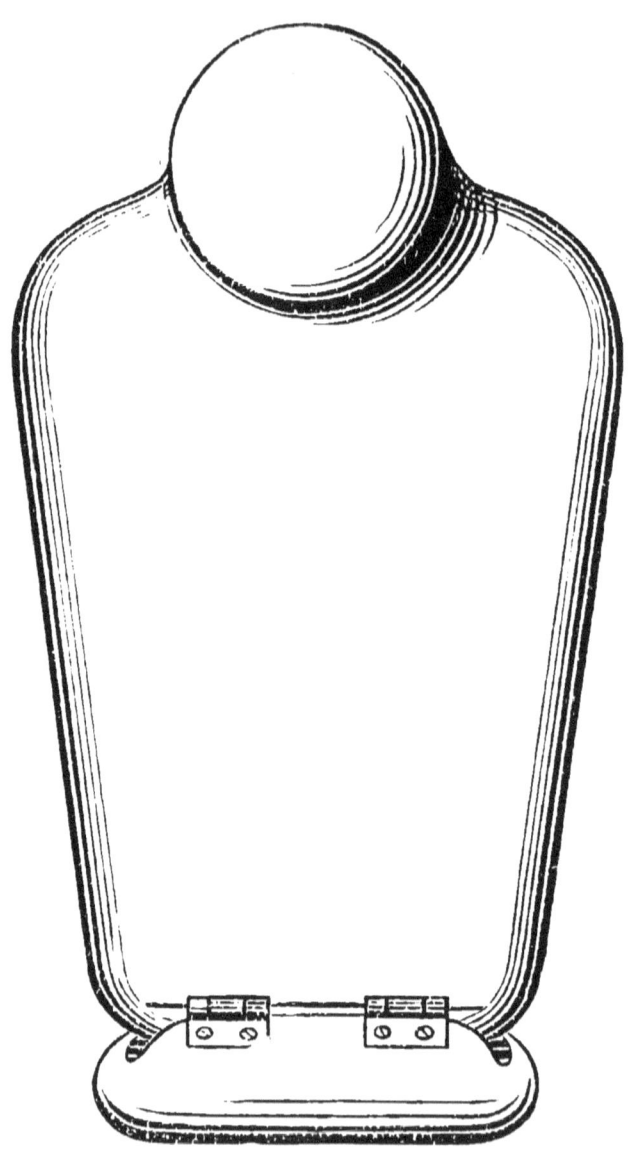

THE SELF-ADJUSTING SHIRT BOARD.

11.—HOW TO USE THE SHIRT BOARD.

BUTTON or pin the shirt band in the back, before inserting the board in the shirt. Raise the clamp at the foot of the board, and holding the shirt bosom taut, smooth out the body of the shirt underneath the clamp, and catch it in the corner recesses; now lower the clamp, and the shirt bosom will be held even and in place, entirely free from wrinkles. Do not be afraid of tearing the shirt. Make the board stretch out every wrinkle. It cannot tear the shirt, as the strain is even over the whole front, far more so than when stretched with the hands. The agents always teach purchasers of Family Right, how to use the Shirt Board; but the directions here given, will be found convenient for future reference.

12.—CARE OF THE SHIRT BOARD.

THE use of the Shirt Board for ironing, the purpose for which it was intended, will not soil the white covering. It is the laying around where dust can settle on it, that soils it. If laid away in a drawer immediately after using, the covering will keep clean for a long time. The muslin is cut to fit the board, and the edge is not a "ragged edge," but is neatly turned under and fastened with light gimp tacks. When the covering becomes soiled, the tacks may be withdrawn with a case-knife, and the muslin washed and replaced, the same tacks being used. The softness and smoothness of the covered surface of the board admirably adapts it for shirt ironing. It is also very convenient for ironing collars, cuffs, ribbons or any small article.

13.—THE COMBINED CORRUGATED GLOSSING AND MOLDING IRON.

IN glossing starched articles, it is requisite that only a small surface of the glossing iron should come in contact with the fabric, and hence, in most laundries the favorite is the "heel-iron," which is shaped somewhat like an ordinary sad-iron with its heel rounded. To produce the gloss, after the articles are ironed and slightly moistened, the point of the "heel-iron" is elevated, and the article rubbed with the oval part of the iron. To polish with that iron, two separate operations are required; one to smooth with the smooth surface of the iron, and the other to polish with the rounded heel; and to produce a thorough polish, numerous rapid motions are required, with a hard pressure of the heel upon the starched article, while the point of the iron is held in an elevated position, which process is tiresome and straining to the arm of the operator. The Corrugated Glossing Iron, for which United States Letters Patent were granted, Dec. 3rd, 1878, is destined to take the precedence of all other glossing irons. It is of recent invention, but in some of the leading laundries, where it has been introduced, it gives the highest satisfaction. The face of the iron is corrugated, or in other words, is composed of alternate oval heels or ridges, and oval grooves, running across the iron parallel to each other. The grooves are open at each end, thereby entirely separating the ridges from each other. Thus each heel produces its own gloss, independently of the other.

14.—ADVANTAGES OF THE CORRUGATED GLOSSING IRON.

ITS chief advantage is, the articles do not have to be ironed previous to its use, but it will smooth and polish at the same time. A shirt front is finished in one operation, thus saving time. Again, it does not require hard pressure, but can be used all day without tiring the operator. In using this iron, the entire corrugated face rests on the starched fabric, avoiding the strain upon the arm, produced in holding the point or heel

The Combined Corrugated Glossing and Molding Iron.

of the iron in an elevated position, as required in using other polishing irons; and each one of the numerous surfaces of this iron, produces at each motion of the iron, an effect equal to the effect of the entire one-surface iron, and hence it is readily seen, that this iron will polish about as much by a single motion, as a one-surface iron will polish by as many motions as there are separate polishing surfaces upon this iron, the smoothing and glossing being performed at the same time and by the same part of the iron. The principle of glossing is the same as in the use of the "heel-iron;" but the tiresome disadvantages of the latter, are entirely overcome. The iron is provided with a collar molder, composed of a double heel, the object of which is to twist the collars and cuffs so as to give them a perfect fit. The iron is also provided with a corrugated or rounded point, to faciliate the polishing of the small surfaces around the collars and bands of shirts, and between the plaits, accessible only to the point of the iron. The ends of the corrugations forming the longitudinal edges of the face of the iron, are rounded, to prevent catching, wearing, or cutting the goods.

15.—HOW TO OPERATE THE CORRUGATED GLOSSING IRON.

AFTER the shirt has been adjusted on the board, as in (11,) smooth it with the corrugated Glossing Iron just like an ordinary sad-iron would be used, and a fine gloss will be imparted to the shirt, with the expenditure of no more time or trouble than when done up in the usual way. After the shirt is stretched over the board it is an improvement to rub the bosom, previous to using the iron, with a clean white towel dampened with soft water. To gloss other starched articles, collars, cuffs, etc., spread them out smoothly on the ironing table, and after rubbing out the wrinkles with the wet towel, iron them with the Glossing Iron. Even where articles are washed and ironed out of the house, they may be glossed just as well after they are returned. In that case, place the articles upon the hard surface of the board, slightly moisten them with soft water, and iron them over with the Glossing Iron, and they will receive a fine polish. If the article has been done up for months, it makes no difference, for a gloss may always be imparted.

16.—EXTRA FINE GLOSS.

IF an extra fine polish be desired, instead of using the wet towel mentioned above, rub the surface to be polished with a sponge dipped in a weak Gum-Arabic solution, prepared as in (28,) and then the Corrugated Iron will produce a superb finish. The article should be only lightly sponged. Purchasers of Family Right will be shown by the agent, a practical use of the corrugated Glossing Iron.

17.—MOLDING COLLARS AND CUFFS.

MOLDING or twisting collars and cuffs, is the process of giving them a round shape, whereby the collar neatly fits the neck, and the cuff the wrist. A collar or cuff is never sent out from a first-class laundry, without being thus molded. The operation is performed altogether with the heel of the iron, and the fit is much more perfect than when shaped with the hands. When these articles are ironed out flat and afterwards shaped with the hands, wrinkles cannot be avoided. Molding a collar is easy to accomplish; but to do it skillfully may require a little practice. The process, however, is much facilitated by the use of the curved double heel of the Corrugated Glossing Iron, the mode of using which is as follows: Any lady, by a little practice, may become an expert in molding collars.

18.—HOW TO OPERATE THE COLLAR MOLDER.

THE article is first ironed and glossed, then in using the double heel, the collar or cuff to be molded, ed, is arranged with one end toward the operator, and the point of the iron in the same direction. The lower rounded surface of the heel is pressed with one hand upon the farther end of the collar, for example; and as the iron is drawn toward the operator, the farther end of the collar is drawn by the other hand in the same direction, over the upper rounded surface of the heel, which process, with the aid of the heat of the iron, curls the collar into the required shape. Cuffs are molded in the same way; and it is found that the separate rounded surfaces or double heel, operate better in this molding process, than one continuous curve or single heel. Collars that are very stiff, can thus be molded to as perfect a fit as could be desired. In the case of standing collars, if the heel of the iron is pressed upon the tips of the collar by one hand, and then the iron drawn toward the operator, and at the same time, the collar drawn in the same direction with the other hand, the tips or points of the collar may be rolled over; and when worn, the points will curve out from the neck of the wearer, and look more artistic than when turned over square. Turn down collars should be first folded over with the fingers, and then molded with the iron. Ladies collars and cuffs should always be molded, as well as those of gentlemen, for no collar or cuff looks or sets well, unless properly molded.

19.—LAUNDRY STYLE OF FOLDING SHIRTS.

THIS is a very neat way of folding shirts, and to some ladies may be of considerable interest. In this style of folding, the cuffs can never get wrinkled or creased; and it is also very convenient when shirts are packed for the journey, as they can thus folded, be laid away in a very small space. Lay the shirt with the bosom downward upon the table, and fold both sides over the back, but instead of folding the sleeves parallel with the sides, as is usually done, lay them out transversely, at right angles to the front. Now bring the body of the shirt up over the sides. Take one sleeve and fold it directly back, sideways, over the body of the shirt, and turning, lay it down lengthwise with the front, folding the cuff over the base of the bosom. Serve the other sleeve and cuff in the same manner; thus the cuffs lay over the base of the bosom, and cannot get wrinkled. Place a pin through the back and sleeves, at the apex of the angle formed by the upper portions of the sleeves; this will hold the folds even and in place. If each fold be compactly pressed down with a warm iron, a dozen shirts folded in this style, may be placed in a box of the length and width of the bosom, and only five inches in height, and neither the bosom nor the cuffs can get wrinkled or creased.

20.—CARE OF SAD-IRONS.

MANY housekeepers are forever vexed with smutty and rusty sad-irons. Every time ironing day comes around, much time and patience is wasted in cleaning irons, before they are fit to use. The question occurs, why do sad-irons rust? Look how they are usually left laying about in the damp and rain, or wherever it happens. Treated in this way, any iron or steel instrument will corrode. A carpenter would be beside himself if his tools were thrown about in so careless a manner. How does he always keep them bright and polished? surely not by letting them care for themselves. He frequently oils them, and keeps them in a dry place. If ladies would only take a similar care of sad-irons, if they would oil them after using, and lay them away in a dry place, the surface of the irons would keep free from rust. The oil will not soil the clothes; for after the iron is heated and rubbed with a dry cloth, no trace of the oil remains. Irons cared for in this manner, in addition to keeping free from rust, will iron much more smoothly.

21.—SCOURING SAD-IRONS.

IN using sad-irons, portions of the starch are liable to adhere to the iron, and the best way of cleaning them, is to scour them with Unburnt Brick. Procure some Unburnt Brick, (the same as is used for scouring knives and forks,) powder it and spread it out over brown paper, and then rub the iron over it. Sad-irons should never be heated on a stove where all kinds of cooking is in process, for the irons are almost sure to get smutted. Before setting on the irons, always clean and well brush the stove. It is a convenient plan to always have on the ironing table, a piece of yellow Beeswax tied up in a coarse cloth. When the iron is almost hot enough to use, but not quite, rub it quickly with the Beeswax cloth, and then with a clean dry cloth. The Corrugated Glossing Iron, although polished and case-hardened, like steel, will rust and corrode if exposed to the damp; but if oiled after using, and put in a dry place, it will never tarnish. Sawdust, Bran and Salt, are all good for cleaning irons.

22.—SAD-IRONS DEEPLY RUST-EATEN

FREQUENTLY sad-irons become so badly rust-eaten, as to appear entirely ruined, but no iron was ever so badly scaled or incrusted with oxide, that it could not be cleaned by the following method :—Immerse the iron for a few minutes, in a solution of one part of concentrated Sulphuric Acid, to ten parts of water. On withdrawing the iron, dip it in a bath of hot Lime water, and hold it there until it becomes so heated, that it will immediately dry on being taken out. Afterward, rub the iron with dry Bran or Sawdust, and it will be chemically clean. Paradoxical as it may seem, strong Sulphuric Acid will not attack iron, with anything of the energy of a solution of the same. In handling Concentrated Sulphuric Acid, be careful not to let it come in contact with the hands or clothing.

23.—NON-CONDUCTING HOLDER.

A SAD-IRON holder that will not easily conduct heat will be found very convenient in the laundry. Such a holder may be prepared of several folds of cloth, with the inside lined with leather. The outside will be soft for the hands, and the leather will keep the holder much cooler than it would otherwise be. A holder of this description, made in leisure moments, will last for years, and saves the bother of hunting paper or rags at every ironing. It has been the aim, by scattering these simple hints throughout the Chemical Laundry Guide, to impress the fact that it is a vast saving of time in the long run, to have everything connected with the laundry exact, handy and neat. By being a trifle precise, far better work will be done, and the drudgery of the laundry will be converted into a pleasure. The main secret of the perfection attained by large laundries, is the neatness, order and system which prevail throughout every department.

24.—TO PRESERVE CLOTHES PINS AND LINES.

CLOTHES PINS are inexpensive articles, and their preservation may appear of little account, yet old clothes pins that have been properly preserved, are much superior to new ones. They will more firmly fasten the clothes upon the line; and the discouraging sight of the clothes lying in the dirt, which not unfrequently greets a lady after a tiresome washing, will be avoided. If every month or so, clothes pins are boiled a few minutes, and then quickly dried, they become more flexible and durable. Clothes lines also will last longer and keep in better order, if occasionly treated in the same manner.

CHAPTER II.

25.—VARIOUS STARCHES AND THEIR USE.

COMMERCIAL starch for laundry purposes, is usually made from wheat or rice. Poland starch is considered superior to the American or English. There are several kinds of domestic starch which may be made in various ways, and of a variety of substances. They each have their peculiar merits and special uses. Starch for linen glossing has been fully treated in (7), and among the most important of home-made starches are the following:—

26.—POTATO STARCH.

A KNOWLEDGE of making Potato Starch of a good quality is very important, for this starch has the advantage that it can always be made at home. Wash several good mealy Potatoes, grate them into a pan of clean water, and stir the mixture well. As soon as the thick part subsides to the bottom, pour off all the white water into another vessel, keeping back all the pulp. Again add water to the pulp and pour off the whitened water as before, repeating this process as long as the water comes off whitish. Let all the whitened water that has been poured off remain undisturbed for some time, and the white part will settle to the bottom, leaving the water quite clear. This subsided matter is the starch. Pour off the water and dry the starch in the sun. The starch will generally weigh about one-fifth of the Potatoes used, if they are of the best quality.

27.—TO MAKE GOOD FLOUR STARCH.

THE manner of making Flour Starch presented in this method is the quickest way it can be prepared; the starch will be of excellent quality, and the method is much better than the old way of preparing Flour Starch by washing dough. Mix sifted Flour gradually with cold water to free it from lumps, and then stir in cold water until the mixture will pour easily. Next stir it into a pot of boiling water, and let it boil five or six minutes, stirring it frequently. A little Lard will make it iron smoother. Strain through muslin. This Starch answers very well for both cottons and linens.

28.—GUM-ARABIC STARCH.

PROCURE two ounces of white Gum-Arabic, and reduce it to a powder. Place the powder in a pitcher, and pour over it boiling soft water—a pint or more, according to the degree of strength desired. Let it remain over night to settle, and in the morning pour it from the dregs into a clean bottle, cork it, and save for use. This starch is used for silks and muslins, and will impart to lawns a newness when nothing else can restore them after washing. It is also excellent for starching thin white muslins and bobbinets, and makes a delicate sizing for silk ribbons and trimmings.

Gum-Arabic Starch may be diluted with water, when desirable to have a weak solution.

29.—STARCH FOR COLORED ARTICLES.

DISSOLVE and add to every pint of starch, while boiling, a piece of Roche Alum the size of a thimble. By so doing, the colors will keep brighter for a longer time, which is very desirable where dresses or other articles of lively colors are often washed, and the trouble is but trifling.

30.—GLUE STARCH.

GLUE Starch is much used for stiffening printed goods of various material. It makes an excellent sizing, and gives a finish as well as stiffness to the goods. Boil a piece of glue four inches square, in four quarts of water, and keep it in a bottle well corked.

31.—ISINGLASS STARCH.

DISSOLVE two ounces of Isinglass flakes in a quart of water, and bottle for use. Isinglass makes a delicate sizing for silk ribbons and fine trimmings. It is the favorite sizing of the French laundress, and its excellence is now familiar to the best milliners and dressmakers of this country. As a sizing for delicate articles, it cannot be excelled.

32.—WATER-PROOF STARCH.

THIS is a patent French method employed in Paris. It consists in passing the goods, after being properly starched, through a bath of Chloride of Zinc, at a temperature of about 60° Fahr. After several successive washings the starch will still remain in the fabric. This method is valuable in cases where starched articles are a great deal exposed to moisture.

33.—NEW PROCESS OF RENDERING CLOTH WATER-PROOF.

FABRICS may be rendered water-proof by this method, without destroying their ventilating qualities. Place in a metal vessel of about six gallons capacity, twenty pounds of Sulphate of Alumina cut in thin slices, and in another similar receptacle, three pounds of Oleic Acid and six quarts of Alcohol. Thoroughly dissolve the latter compound, and stir it with a wooden stick for twenty minutes, gradually adding the Sulphate of Alumina. Leave the whole about twenty-four hours to settle; the Oleic Acid and the Alcohol will then be at the surface, and can be decanted. Filter the remaining deposit through flannel, and press it into a cake. This cake can be dried by heat and then powdered. One and a half pounds of the powder to twenty gallons of water, will be an ample proportion for applying to silken or linen clothes, and wool will not require more than one pound. It is well to strain the solution. The articles require only to be thoroughly saturated with this solution and dried in the air. This method has been awarded a patent.

34.—CONGREE STARCH FOR MUSLINS.

SOAP may be disused in the getting up of fine muslins, by treating them agreeably to the Oriental custom, which consists in washing them in plain water, and then boiling them in Congree or rice water. After which, they ought not to be submitted to the operation of the smoothing iron, but should be rubbed smooth with a glass bottle containing hot water (231.) The water in which Rice is boiled without being tied up in a bag, is as good as Poland starch, for clear starching muslins. After it is poured off from the rice, the water should be boiled till it evaporates to a thick consistency, and then strained.

35—TO STARCH MUSLINS AND PIQUES

IN laundrying fine muslins and piques, the failure is quite as often in the starching as in the washing. A good sized pailful of starch should be used, in which three or four inches of Stearin Candle has been melted while the starch is hot. The starch should be thoroughly squeezed from the goods, and the articles folded whilst damp, between folds of old sheeting or table-linen. It is a good plan to pass them through the wringing machine, as all lumps of starch will be thus removed. Piques should be ironed as lighty as possible, and the iron ought never to come in contact with the outside surface. When absolutely necessary to iron them on the right side, an old cambric handkerchief is the best to place between the iron and the material. Muslins look very well when starched and clapped dry while the starch is hot; then fold in a damp cloth, until they become quite damp, before ironing them, for if muslins are sprinkled in the usual way, they are quite liable to be spotted.

36.—TO THICKEN AND STRENGTHEN MUSLIN.

DIP the muslin in dilute Sulphuric Acid, which will strengthen it very much, and increase its thickness.

This is the process employed in the factories of Manchester, England. The cotton thus prepared, is technically termed "blanket." The Acid should be quite dilute, and the article should be immersed only for a few minutes, and then rinsed well in clear water.

37.—YELLOW LINEN.

LINEN that has acquired a yellow or bad color by careless washing, may be restored to a brilliant whiteness, if treated according to this method. The process is called in laundries, "The Bleach." It is especially used for shirts, collars and cuffs, and its object is to give them that clear white appearance these articles always possess when done up at a first-class laundry. After the dirt is extracted and the clothes are boiled, they are then put into the "Bleach," which is prepared and used as follows:—

38.—THE LAUNDRY "BLEACH."

TAKE a quarter of a pound of Chloride of Lime, and mix it with sufficient cold water to form a paste. Work the paste entirely free from lumps, put it into a vessel, and add two gallons of boiling water. Allow it to settle, and decant the clear liquid, which is the bleaching fluid. Immerse the article in the liquid for five or six minutes, and then without wringing, put them into water scalding hot, and let them remain about fifteen minutes; this is done to neutralize the effect of the Chloride of Lime upon the linen. If this precaution is not taken, the texture of the goods will be injured. Never attempt to bleach unwashed linen; and avoid using the liquor too strong, for the action of the " Bleach," is very powerful, and if the linen is left in too long, it will be rendered rotten. Great care must be taken. Notwithstanding the powerful action of the " Bleach," experience has given abundant proof that it will not injure the goods in the least, if properly used. This process is in use in nearly every laundry establishment, and is regarded as indispensable in giving clothes a clear, brilliant whiteness. The " Bleach " will also remove almost any kind of stain, except iron mould.

39.—TO BLEACH BROWN SHEETING.

FIRST soak the clothes for twelve hours in strong soap suds. For every twelve yards of sheeting, take a quarter of a pound of Chloride of Lime and dissolve it in enough boiling water, so that when immersed in the liquid, the cloth may be entirely covered. As soon as soon as the Lime is dissolved, strain the solution through a coarse cloth; then put the brown sheeting in the strained Lime water, stirring it continually, and after it has remained thus in the liquid for half an hour, take out the cloth and rinse it well in boiling water, to remove all the Lime water. Then boil it up in strong soap-suds, and hang out to dry. The work of weeks of grass bleaching will thus be accomplished in a day.

40.—GERMAN METHOD OF BLEACHING WHITE GOODS.

THIS method consists in employing Oil of Turpentine as a bleaching agent. It is a favorite and extensively used method throughout Germany; and before American manufacturers learned the proper way of bleaching, they were compelled to send certain kinds of goods to Germany, to be bleached. The German method possesses a great advantage over other methods, for there is no danger of the goods being injured. Dissolve one part Oil of Turpentine in three parts strong Alcohol. Place a teacupful of this mixture in the water used for the last rinsing; the clothes are to be rinsed in this, well wrung out, and hung in the open air to dry. The bleaching action of the Oil consists in its changing Oxygen into Ozone when exposed to the light, and in the process of drying, the Turpentine disappears, leaving no trace behind.

41.—TO STARCH AND IRON WHITE VESTS.

PREPARE the starch for fine white vests, the same as for shirts (7.) After dipping the vest in the hot starch, lay it on a clean hard surface, and with the hands work the adhering starch well into the vest, at the same time drawing it into proper shape, and smoothing out the wrinkles. Let it dry in this shape, and instead of sprinkling, place it without rolling up, between damp sheets. When damp enough to iron, first pull the vest into its proper shape, and smooth out the wrinkles with a damp cloth; then having underneath the vest a very soft ironing surface, do not apply the iron directly on the vest, but place over it a damp cloth, and press the cloth till quite dry. In this way the twills and flowers will be brought out clear and distinct as they are when new, and the vest will have a proper shape.

42.—RAISED EMBROIDERY AND FLOWERED COLLARS.

THE surface on which any kind of embroidered work is ironed should be very soft—composed of a number of folds of flannel. Stretch out the article smoothly and lay it on this soft surface with the right side downward, and then press heavily with the iron on the wrong side. The soft flannel allows the raised portions to sink down, and the flowers and embroidery will not be all pressed together, but will have a clear outline. New linen may be embroidered more easily by rubbing it over with fine white soap, which will prevent the thread from cracking.

43.—DOING UP LACE CURTAINS.

DOUBLE the curtain lengthwise, and tack the ends together with a needle and thread, this being done so that the curtain may easily handled in the water. Prepare a strong lather of white soap and water, and add one ounce of Aqua Ammonia. Soap should never be rubbed on the curtain, nor should the material itself be rubbed; sluicing it up and down in the suds will answer quite as well, and does not tear it to pieces. Continue to wash the curtain through successive lathers, until the last one does not appear dirty. Rinse through several waters with a little Blueing or Rose Pink (63) in the last. They may be starched to any degree of stiffness that may suit the taste. Many ladies attempt to iron lace curtains; but this is folly.

They should always be stretched tight and thus allowed to dry. Either stretch them tightly over quilting frames, or, having tacked a clean white sheet over the floor of an occupied room, stretch the curtain tightly over it, and fasten with pins. This is the only correct way of doing up lace curtains.

44.—LADIES' LINEN SUITS.

LINENS properly laundried are elegant summer costumes; but to most ladies, the art of preserving the new appearance of linen suits is very perplexing. Many ladies try to be so careful, that they may wear them the whole season without soiling them, for they are well aware that, when once washed, the color and lustre disappears. The suits most in vogue are of a hay, straw or amber color. They are made on machines by factory girls, and are then sent to the laundries to be given the color and finish. The methods employed are easy to follow; the lustre and almost any color desired may be readily given them. For example, if a hay color be desired, take some Hay and steep it just as tea is steeped; and after the suit is washed and rinsed, it is immersed in this Hay tea, which will give the hay color. The lustre is imparted while the linen is being ironed. Prepare a sizing as follows:—Dissolve bought starch in cold water, using just enough water to convert it, by rubbing between the fingers, into a paste entirely free from lumps; then add soap water to this creamy starch or paste, until the mixture is quite thin. Do not add soap-suds, but a soap solution, prepared by simply dissolving white soap in hot water. Then, while ironing, lightly dampen a portion of the suit with this sizing, and immediately iron dry the moistened portion. Continue thus until the whole suit is ironed, and the result will be a fine glossy finish. If a straw color be desired, steep Straw into a tea; if an amber color, obtain some Amber and prepare an Amber tea or solution. Almost any color that may suit the taste may be imparted by steeping a tea of some substance of similar color, and dressing the suit with it. The lustre is always added by using the soap and starch sizing, as above.

45.—IRONING AND FOLDING TABLE LINENS.

IN ironing table linens, there is quite a knack in folding them so that they may be conveniently spread over the table, and the creases caused by the folds may not be visible. The snowy table cloth looks much neater, if it presents a smooth even surface. The creases so often seen in the table cloth, which is otherwise faultlessly done up, are too suggestive of the heat of the laundry. By observing the accompanying directions for ironing and folding table linens, a pleasing result will follow. Only one side, of course, need be smoothed. First fold the table cloth the long way, with the right side in, then bring both the outer edges even with the middle crease, thus exposing for smoothing half of the right side, a fourth above and a fourth underneath. Now smooth all of the right side which is exposed above and underneath. Next bring over both of these new creases even with the middle crease, thereby exposing to the iron another portion of the right side above and underneath. Iron these portions. The middle crease is now reversed, which brings the last formed creases even with each other, and the remaining unironed portion of the right side above and underneath will be exposed for ironing. All of the right side is now ironed, and the table cloth is in eight folds, lengthwise. Finish by folding it crosswise, and bringing the outer edges even with the middle crease. The table cloth will now be smoothed and folded in a very convenient form, for spreading over the table; and when spread out, the creases will disappear. This is also a good way of folding napkins and handkerchiefs.

CHAPTER III.

46.—WASHING.

THROUGHOUT the world, wherever man dwells, water is used for cleansing purposes. Previous to its use, however, it may itself require to be cleansed. The impurities of water are of two kinds. Earthy matter, clay, sand, lime, &c., mechanically suspended in it, which makes it appear cloudy and turbid. Then, again, dissolved substances, which contaminate and render the water hard, although it may appear clear and pure.

In order to have clothes clear and soft after washing, it is highly imperative that the water used should itself be free from all impurities. The surest way to clarify turbid water is by filtration. The principles of filtration are very simple, and are universally understood. Any box or cask will answer, and Charcoal is the usual material through which to filter the water. The foulest ditch water, made to pass through Charcoal, comes out clear, bright and sweet.

47.—SPONGY IRON FOR FILTERING WATER.

IT is confidently stated by chemists that the best filter for impure water is Spongy Iron. Bacteria and germs are not killed by being passed through Charcoal, but are destroyed by filtering through Spongy Iron. The organic matter is destroyed by the oxygen liberated by the iron from the water, and the ferrous hydrate resulting from the solution by organic matter is re-oxidized by the oxygen dissolved in the water, so that the process of purification is a continous one, and the Spongy Iron is not destroyed by the operation.

48.—POPULAR METHODS OF CLEARING WATER.

MANY steamboats on the Ohio and Mississippi Rivers clear the dirty river water by adding ground Mustard to it and allowing it to settle. In England and France, as well as in America, a popular method of clearing muddy water is to add a few grains of powdered Alum to it. Two or three grains are usually sufficient for a quart of water. This will effectually clear the water, but at the same time it augments the hardness of the water by altering its chemical composition. By far the superior way is by the following method:

49.—EGG AND VINEGAR METHOD.

BEAT an Egg and three tablespoonfuls of Vinegar together. Stir this mixture into a tubful of the muddy water, and let it remain undisturbed until the impurities of the water, together with the Egg mixture, settle to the bottom in a yellowish and very dirty sediment. Decant the water from this sediment, and it will be as clear and pure as spring water. This is a simple and very valuable method.

50.—HARD WATER.

WATER that is hard and unfit for cleansing purposes, on account of the dissolved impurities it may contain, will be now considered. Many people use Pearlash, or Potash to soften hard water, but these ingredients are apt to injure the cloth. The method given below cannot be too highly recommended. Water softened by this process cannot injure the finest goods nor the most delicate of colors, and it will render the clothes clearer and softer than when washed in rain water. It is also very nice for washing the skin, or for any cleansing purpose whatever. It is a costless and easy method. Water thus softened is usually termed "Broke-Water."

51.—METHOD OF PREPARING "BROKE-WATER."

FILL a tub or barrel half full of wood ashes. Hickory ashes are the best, but any wood ashes will answer, and sometimes even coal ashes are used. Sift the ashes through a fine sieve, to separate any black coals they may contain, as these will give the "Broke-Water," or lye, a blackish hue. Next fill up the tub with water, and allow it to stand over night. If hot water be used, half an hour will answer. From half a gallon to a gallon of this "Broke-Water," put into a boiler of hot but not boiling water, will cause the impurities of the water to rise to the surface in a milky skum, which may be easily skimmed off, and the water underneath will be as clear as the purest spring water. When the liquid is all used, more water can be poured on the same ashes, and thus the "Broke-Water" may be prepared whenever it is wanted. Every family that has been accustomed to use hard water should try this method.

52.—WASHING CRYSTAL.

MANY people have a strong prejudice against the use of any preparation except soap to aid in taking the dirt out of clothes. They say it eats the cloth and turns it yellow. In the case of many of the so-called washing crystals in market, this prejudice is just; yet chemistry would be but a meagre science if it could not give a preparation which would be successful in extracting dirt from linen and cotton, and combine it in such proportions that it would be entirely harmless. In laundry establishments, washing fluids are universally used, resulting in a great saving of labor and time, and proving far less destructive to wearing apparel than the old mode of washing. Surely, any method which saves labor and time, and accomplishes better results than the old plan, ought to be introduced into the family. Look at the advantages: No rubbing the skin off the hands, nor tearing the clothes to pieces; a large washing finished before breakfast, the clothes out to dry, the house in good order, all comfortable again for the day, and the family saved from washing day annoyances. Surely, no family can forego such comforts.

Another great advantage in the use of washing compounds, which should not be overlooked, is the small amount of soap that will be required for a washing. A good washing crystal will do away with more than one-half the soap that without it would be necessary. The quantity of soap saved every year by this means is an item of no small importance.

Several plans of washing that are in use in large laundries, and a few formulæ for preparing the best washing crystals, are presented. All of them are valuable methods, and none will injure the goods in the least. A lady may select whichever one is most convenient.

53.—PROF. TWELVETREE'S METHOD.

THE plan of washing largely in use in England is called "The Recipe of Prof. Twelvetree." It has an advantage in the use of the lime, which possesses strong bleaching properties, and will render the clothes beautifully white. By this method the finest laces, linens, cambrics, &c., can be readily cleansed, with little trouble.

On the night previous to washing, select from the clothes to be washed all the coarse and dirty pieces, separating them from the fine. Then soak both lots over night, in separate tubs of soft water. Next, the liquid for a large washing is prepared as follows: Put in another tub half a pound of good brown Soap, finely sliced, half a pound of Soda and three ounces of fresh, unslaked Lime. Mix them all together, and add one gallon of boiling soft water. Stir the mixture well to thoroughly incorporate the ingredients, and let it stand till morning. Then strain off the clear liquid, but be careful to leave all sediment behind. Having ready in the boiler about ten gallons of boiling soft water, pour in the prepared liquid, keeping back all settlings that may yet remain in it. Then throw in the clothes and boil them about twenty minutes or half an hour. It is a good plan to put an earthen plate in the bottom of the boiler to prevent the clothes from burning. After boiling the clothes the allotted time, take them out, scald them, blue them, and rinse them in clear soft water, and they will then be as clear and white as snow. If the washing be small, and less than ten gallons of water be required in which to boil the clothes, less in proportion of the liquid of Lime, Soap and Soda should be used. In the country, where it is difficult to procure fresh Lime, a large quantity of the liquid can be prepared at one time. Preserved in bottles, tightly corked, it will keep for years, always ready for use.

54.—AN EXCELLENT DETERGENT FLUID.

THE following washing fluid has proven very successful: Take two and a half pounds of Salsoda, half a pound of Borax, quarter of a pound of unslaked Lime, two ounces of Salts of Tartar, and one and a half ounce of Liquid Ammonia. Dissolve the Soda and Borax in half a gallon of hot water. Let it settle, and when clear pour it off carefully. Then add the other ingredients, and turn upon the whole four gallons of cold water. The fluid is now ready for use, and should be kept in a cask or jug. The night before washing, take six tablespoonfuls to a tubful of clothes, mixing it with four pailfuls of warm water. Soak the clothes over night. Next morning add hot water enough to wash them with good soap-suds. Then boil the clothes. Another tubful of clothes may be washed in the same water used for the first boiler. One trial of this fluid will show its good effects. The recipe has been sold at a high price, and a great deal of money has been made out of the manufacture of this fluid.

55.—BORAX WASHING CRYSTAL.

THE washerwomen of Holland and Belgium, so proverbially clean, and who get their linen so beautifully white, use Borax instead of Soda for a washing crystal. Many laundries have adopted this method. It is used in the proportion of half a pound of Borax powder to ten gallons of water. This method will save the Soap nearly one-half. For laces, cambrics, &c., an extra quantity of Borax is used. For crinolines, requiring to be very stiff, a still stronger solution is necessary. Borax is a neutral salt, and will not injure the finest fabric. It is also good to soften hard water, and is excellent for the toilet.

56.—FRENCH WASHING COMPOUND.

THIS compound is used by French laundresses, and is now largely employed by laundries in this country. It will be found very effectual, and entirely harmless. Dissolve one pound of hard Soap in six gallons of water, then add a quarter of an ounce of Spirits of Turpentine and half an ounce of Spirits of Hartshorn. The above quantity is sufficient for a medium-sized washing.

57.—JAVELLE WATER.

IT is very convenient to always have on hand in the family the celebrated Javelle Water, small quantities of which will render the most soiled garments perfectly white. It should be used only in small quantities. It is prepared by taking four pounds of Salsoda to one pound of Chloride of Lime and one gallon of water. Put the Salsoda into a vessel placed over the fire, and add a gallon of boiling water. Let it boil about fifteen minutes. Next, make the Chloride of Lime free from lumps and add it to the Soda solution. When cool, pour the solution into a large jug or bottle, cork tightly, and it will keep, always ready for use. The materials are cheap, and the mixture easily made.

58.—VEGETABLE COLORS.

IT is hardly necessary to remind ladies that none of these washing or bleaching preparations should be used in doing up colored articles. Although they do not injure the fabric, they are apt to bleach out and destroy vegetable colors. Neither should they be used with woolens and flannels, as they will render such materials harsh. For white goods only can they be profitably employed.

59.—ASSORTING CLOTHES.

IN large washes, much labor and soap can be saved by assorting the clothes and soaking them over night, previous to washing them. In assorting the wash, put the flannels in one lot, the colored goods in another, the coarse white clothes in another, and the fine white articles in a fourth. Wash the fine white clothes first, the coarse white articles in the same water, and then wash the colored goods. The skilful treatment of flannels and colored articles will be fully given in chapters appropriated to them.

It is a good plan to save the suds, after washing, to water the garden, or to harden sandy yards or cellars.

60.—BLUEING.

A GREAT deal of vexation is experienced by housewives in the use of blueing. Many blues settle on the clothes in spots and render them streaked. The object of blueing clothes is to clear them and give them a bright look. Articles properly blued will look as fresh and bright as when they were new. The chief requisite of a good blueing is the ability to diffuse itself throughout the rinse water, and to always remain in solution, the whole water being thoroughly blued, and no particle of the blue remaining undissolved to settle on the clothes. Aniline Blue possesses this property, and is the blue usually preferred by laundries. It is considered superior to others.

61.—ANILINE BLUE.

TAKE two ounces of Aniline Blue to half a gallon of clear water. Tepid water is the best. Let the Blue dissolve thoroughly, and put the solution away in bottles. The above quantity will last for some time. Use in the rinse water from a teaspoonful to a table spoonful, according to the size of the washing. The proper quantity to be used can be readily determined by the appearance of the water. Clothes do not require so very much blueing, nor yet too little. They may have a decidedly blue appearance while wet, but in the process of ironing and drying the excess of blue disappears, and a brilliant white remains. Nothing can excel the pure Aniline Dye for blueing clothes, and such is its strength that it is the cheapest that can be used.

62.—CHINESE SOLUBLE BLUE.

CHINESE Soluble Blue also makes an elegant blueing for laundry use. It is prepared and used in the same manner, and in the same proportions, as the Aniline Blue (61). It is a blue powder exceedingly soluble, and, when once dissolved in water, it forms a clear, permanent blue liquid, entirely free from sediment. It is not even necessary to shake it before using.

63.—ROSE PINK.

THE French laundress very frequently employs Rose Pink instead of blueing to clear delicate articles. It is considered much superior to blueing for fine muslins, laces, and various silk goods, as it will impart to delicate articles a very bright and beautiful appearance. Rose Pink may be procured of the chemist, and is used in the same way as the Indigo Blue. Tie up a small quantity in a piece of flannel, and squeeze drops of the Pink into the water until it is colored a pale pink. We would recommend ladies to try Rose Pink whenever they may have occasion for doing up delicate white articles.

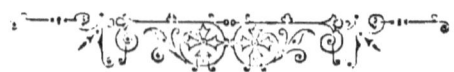

CHAPTER IV.

64.—SOAP OF DOMESTIC MANUFACTURE.

"THE quantity of Soap consumed by a nation would be no inaccurate measure whereby to estimate its wealth and civilization." This remark of Leibig, uttered centuries ago, is as true to-day. Soap is indispensable to every human being. The manufacture of Soap is strictly scientific, and a complete treatise would fill volumes. This work will give only a few methods for the domestic manufacture of Soap, whereby an excellent quality of soft, hard and toilet Soaps, can be easily made, with economy, at home. To those ladies who delight to experiment and improve upon old methods, this chapter is especially devoted.

65.—SOFT SOAPS.

SOAP is a chemical combination of some fatty substance with Caustic Lye. Soft soap differs from hard soap in having Potash as its alkaline base, instead of Soda. It is more or less pasty and gelatinous. Manufacturers of commercial soft soap obtain Lye from Potash, but in domestic manufacture it is usually supplied by Ashes. To make good soap, it is essential at the outset to understand how to make good Lye. In the following method a few hints are given which may be of service:

66.—TO MAKE GOOD LYE.

WHEN it is not desirable to use Potash, hickory Ashes are the best for making Lye, but those made from sound beech, maple, or almost any kind of hard wood, will answer. A common barrel set upon an inclined platform makes a very good leach. A better way is to make a box or trough in a V shape, having its sides terminating in a point, and provided with an orifice at the lower end. The box should be provided with legs, and mounted high enough to allow of a vessel being placed underneath to receive the Lye which runs out of the bottom. This style of leach is much preferable; for the strength of the Ashes is better obtained, and the box may be taken apart and laid away when not in use. First put in the bottom of the leach a few sticks, and spread over them a piece of carpet or woolen cloth, which is better than straw. After a few inches of Ashes have been put in, add from four to eight quarts of Lime. As you fill up with Ashes, moisten and tamp them down well. Tamp the firmest in the centre. It is difficult to obtain the full strength of Ashes in a barrel without removing them after a few days' leaching, when they should be well mixed up and replaced. First, throw off the top, and add new Ashes to make up the proper quantity. It is best to use boiling water for the second leaching. The Lye must be concentrated by boiling till sufficiently strong to float an egg or sound potato.

67.—TO PRESERVE GREASE.

THE proper care and treatment of the fat or grease is very important, and the extra attention given to this matter will be well repaid by the superior quality of soap that will result from the purified grease. Boil all the scraps, rinds and bones in a weak lye, and the purer grease in clear water. After the mixture cools, take off the cake of grease and strain it. It is well to thus occasionally treat the fat as it is saved; for, when kept a long time impure grease becomes offensive. Before consigning it to the grease-tub, care must be taken to dry off all the water, so that the grease will keep sweet. The best way to collect dripping is to put the grease while warm into water that is nearly cold. Any impurities it may contain will sink to the bottom.

68.—TO PREVENT FATTY SUBSTANCES FROM TURNING RANCID.

BOIL, for ten minutes, about eight pounds of the fat with three pounds of water, containing half an ounce of common Salt and a quarter of an ounce of powdered Alum. Strain off the water, and then gently simmer the clarified fat with half an ounce of Benzoin and a pint of Rose Water. Skim off the grease and let it cool. Fat thus treated will keep sweet for years.

69.—TO MAKE SOFT SOAP BY EMPLOYING POTASH.

FOR a barrel of soap, take twelve pounds of Potash to fourteen pounds of grease. Dissolve the Potash over night in two pailfuls of hot soft water. In the morning, pour it while hot over the grease, which must have been previously rendered down and put in the barrel. Put more water on the Potash that remains undissolved, and, when hot, add it to the grease as before, and so continue until all the Potash has been dissolved. Fill up the barrel more slowly with cold water, finishing it the next day. It should be stirred very frequently through the day, and for several successive days. Before using, allow it to rest for three months in a cool cellar. This method furnishes a very good quality of soft soap.

70.—TO MAKE LYE SOFT SOAP.

TAKE about four gallons of Lye obtained by Method (66) to twelve pounds of clear grease. Boil the grease and lye thoroughly together. Then add more lye as it is obtained, keeping up a slow fire and often stirring, until a barrel of soap is formed. After boiling together the twelve pounds of grease and four gallons of lye, the mixture may then be put in the barrel and the rest of the lye added there. By this cold process good soap will be formed, if frequently stirred. The heating process, however, is the best, if the weather be clear and there be plenty of time.

71.—CONCENTRATED LYE.

A MILD, salvy, soft soap, of excellent quality, and one that will be ready for use in a few days, can be quickly made as follows: A prepared Concentrated Lye, put up in pound boxes, may be purchased of any druggist or grocer, at small cost. In some iron vessel, dissolve a pound of this Lye in two quarts of soft water, and add four pounds of grease, scraps or rinds. Boil the mixture thoroughly until every bit of fat disappears. The longer the boiling is continued, the better will be the soap. Then put it in a barrel and add soft water, well boiled and scalding hot, until the soap is as strong as desired. Special directions usually accompany the boxes of Concentrated Lye.

72.—LABOR-SAVING SOAP.

AN excellent soft soap may be made from the washing crystal of Method' (54). Take one quart of the fluid, slice into it three pounds of common yellow soap, and add two pounds of Salsoda. Boil the mixture in three gallons of soft water, then strain it, and it will be immediately fit for use. Four gallons of soft soap will thus be made, which will prove unequaled for all purposes wherein soft soap is needed. The night previous to washing, put the clothes to soak; and to every pailful of water in which they are boiled add a pound of this soap. They will need no rubbing; merely rinse them, and they will be perfectly clean and white. This soap may be rightly styled Labor-Saving Soap.

73.—TURPENTINE SOAP.

SLICE up three pounds of brown soap, and melt it in seven quarts of water. Then put it in a stone pot, and add nine tablespoonfuls of Spirits of Turpentine and six of Alcohol. In using Turpentine soap, make very hot suds with some of the soap, and soak the clothes in it for half an hour. Then wash them out and rinse as usual. This soap is particularly valuable for blankets and quilts, as it thoroughly removes the dirt with very little rubbing.

74.—TO CONVERT SOFT SOAP INTO HARD SOAP.

PUT four pailfuls of soft soap into a kettle, and, while boiling, stir into it by degrees about a quart of common Salt. Boil until all the water evaporates from the curd, and then draw off the water with a siphon, or by tilting the kettle. Pour the paste into a wooden frame, in which muslin, well powdered with a mixture of Lime and Starch, has been placed. Any wooden box large and tight enough will answer, and the muslin should extend over the sides of the box, so that the soap may be easily lifted out. When the soap becomes firm lift it out, and when nearly dry cut it into bars with a brass wire, and let it harden. A little powdered Resin assists the soap to harden, and gives it a fine yellow color. If the soft soap be very thin, a larger quantity of Salt must be used.

75.—HARD SOAPS.

THE domestic manufacture of hard soaps is attended with no more labor or trouble than is met in the making of soft soaps. A very fine and pure quality of hard soap can be made, without difficulty, at home. The main difference between hard and soft soap is in the alkaline base. The alkaline base of hard soap is Caustic Soda; and the more solid the fat used, the firmer will be the resulting soap.

76.—HOME-MADE CAUSTIC SODA.

DISSOLVE six pounds of common washing Soda in four gallons of warm water. Next, slake six pounds of clean fresh Lime, using only as much water as is needed to perfectly crumble it. Stir the slaked

Lime and the Soda solution together, and add four gallons of boiling water. Stir the mixture thoroughly and let it settle. Then pour off the clear lye for use.

77.—DOMESTIC HARD SOAP.

PUT the Caustic Soda, prepared in the manner and quantity given in Method (76), into a clean iron kettle, and add during continual stirring twelve pounds of clarified fat, dusting in, a little at a time, four ounces of finely powdered Borax. Let the mass gently boil for ten or fifteen minutes, or until it thickens and becomes ropy. Then have in readiness a clean, tight box, lined with a piece of muslin large enough to extend well over the sides, to allow of the contents being afterward conveniently lifted out. Pour the mixture from the kettle into the box, and allow it to stand a few days to harden. When sufficiently hard, turn it out on a table, and cut it into bars with a brass wire. Soap thus made, and left to harden in a cool, dry place, will be hard enough for use in a month.

78.—CONCENTRATED LYE HARD SOAP.

FILL an iron kettle two-thirds full of the concentrated lye of Method (66), and add to it melted fat, a ladleful at a time, stirring constantly till the mixture becomes creamy. Then add Salt in small quantities at a time, stirring without intermission, until a perfect ring can be made on the surface with a stick. Then let the fire go out, and the soap will rise to the surface and harden as it cools. Tilt the kettle to draw the lye from under the soap, or else lift out the soap and lay it where it will dry hard enough to cut into bars.

79.—HARD WHITE TALLOW SOAP.

THIS is a fine white soap, of excellent quality, and is made as follows: Dissolve two pounds of Sal-soda in one gallon of boiling soft water. Mix with it two pounds of fresh slaked Lime, stirring occasionally for several hours. Then let it settle. Pour off the clear liquid and add two pounds of Tallow, and boil the mixture till all the Tallow is dissolved. Cool the paste in a flat box, and when sufficiently firm cut into bars or cakes. It may be scented by stirring in the desired perfume as it cools.

80.—CHEAP FAMILY SOAP.

ADD to ten quarts of water six pounds of Quicklime (Shell Lime is best) and six pounds of common washing Soda. Put all together, and let them stand over night to clear. In the morning, after boiling the mixture for half an hour, draw off the lye, and add to it one pound of common Resin and seven pounds of almost any kind of fat. Boil the mass for half an hour. Let it stand till cool and cut into bars. This kind of soap is largely used in laundry establishments.

81.--MYRTLE SOAP.

DISSOLVE two pounds and a quarter of white Potash in five quarts of water, and add to this solution ten pounds of Myrtle Wax. Boil the whole over a slow fire till it turns to soap. Now add a teacupful of cold water, and boil for ten minutes longer. At the end of that time, turn it into moulds or tin pans, and let it dry for a week or ten days before turning it out of the moulds. It may be scented by stirring into it, just before turning it into the moulds, any essential oil that has an agreeable perfume. This soap is excellent for shaving and for chapped hands. It is also very good for eruptions on the face. It will be fit for use in three or four weeks after it is made, but it is better to let it stand nearly a year before using.

82.—CHEMICAL SOAP.

THIS is an admirable soap for removing grease spots. It is the same soap that has often been peddled throughout the country, and the process of manufacturing it claimed to be so wonderful and secret. It is easily made, however. Take an ounce of Fuller's Earth, and just moisten it with Spirits of Turpentine. Then add one ounce each of Salts of Tartar and the best quality of Potash. Work the whole into a paste with a little soap.

83.—OX GALL SOAP.

GALL soap, so valuable in washing fine silk goods and ribbons, is prepared in the following manner: Heat a pound of Cocoanut Oil in a copper vessel to 60° Fahr., and add to it, during constant stirring, half a pound of Caustic Soda. Heat in another vessel half a pound of white Venetian Turpentine, and when quite hot stir it into the first vessel. Then cover this vessel and gently heat it for four hours, after which time increase the fire till the contents become perfectly clear. Next add a pound of Ox Gall, and then stir into the mixture a sufficient quantity of perfectly dry

Castile Soap to cause the whole mass to yield but little under the pressure of the finger. From one to two pounds of Castile Soap would be required for the above quantity of ingredients. When it cools, cut it into cakes. No soap can be manufactured which can excel the detergent properties of Ox Gall soap. It will not injure the finest colors.

84.—TOILET SOAPS.

THE making of toilet soaps is in reality more simple and easier to accomplish than the manufacture of plain soaps. With very little trouble and expense enough toilet soap can be made at one time to last a family for years. If the directions be strictly followed, toilet soaps can be made at home vastly superior to the average market article. The chief requisite in making toilet soap is neatness. The finer kinds of scented soaps, having emollient properties, are rarely made direct by the perfumer, but have for a base some well selected common white soap, which must be cleansed and purified. To be adapted for perfumery, the base should be perfectly neutral, firm and free from all unpleasant odors. The process employed for refining the body soap is called "Crutching."

85.—"CRUTCHING."

CUT up the soap which has been selected for the base as fine as meal, which fits it to be readily melted. Mix it with Rose and Orange Flower Water in the proportion of half a pint of each to twelve pounds of the soap. As it becomes fluid, stir it thoroughly till the paste becomes uniformly consistent and smooth throughout. For this purpose, the perfumer uses a stick having a cross-piece at one end like an inverted T, or crutch. Hence the term, "Crutching." After the first crutching, allow the paste to cool, and then melt and thoroughly crutch it again, but without using the fragrant water. When the paste begins to cool again, add any desired coloring matter, and lastly the perfume, which is reserved to the last to avoid any loss by evaporation from the hot paste. When cool, put the paste into frames and allow it to harden for a day or two. Then cut it with a brass wire into cakes of any desired shape and size.

Crutching constitutes the principal treatment in making toilet soaps, and it is now only necessary to give the proportions of ingredients for several superb varieties.

86.—HONEY SOAP.

USE for the base five pounds of white curd soap. Melt and crutch it with one pound of white Honey. Then add three ounces of Storax and an ounce and a half of powdered Benzoin. Prepared in the above proportions, it will make a mild and very agreeable soap for toilet use.

87.—MUSK SOAP.

USE for the base three pounds of the best quality of Tallow soap and two pounds of Palm Oil soap. Melt and crutch with powdered Cloves, Pale Roses and Gilliflowers, each half an ounce. Perfume with Essence of Bergamot and Essence of Musk, each half an ounce. Tinge with Spanish Brown, one ounce.

88.—CELEBRATED WINDSOR SOAP.

WINDSOR soap, so celebrated as a toilet article, has for its base fine white curd soap, five pounds; Cocoanut Oil soap, one pound. Perfume with a mixture of Attar of Carraway, two ounces; Attars of Thyme and Rosemary, each half an ounce, and Attars of Cassia and Cloves, each one-fourth of an ounce.

To make the Brown Windsor, add a little yellow soap to the white base, and color with Caromel. The White and Brown Windsor are among the finest toilet soaps that are manufactured.

89.—GLYCERINE SOAP.

USE for a base any mild toilet soap, with which about one-twentieth of its weight of Price's Glycerine has been intimately incorporated while in a melted state. Tinge it of a red or rose color with a little Tincture of Archil or of Dragon's Blood. It is variously scented, but Oil of Bergamot or Rose Geranium, supported with a little Oil of Cassia, is its favorite perfume.

90.—ITALIAN HONEY SOAP.

CUT into thin slices two pounds of good yellow soap. Place it in a double saucepan and keep water boiling around it, stirring it frequently while it melts. Then add a quarter of a pound each of Palm

Oil and Honey, and a little True Oil of Cinnamon. Let all boil together six or eight minutes. Then pour it out and let it stand till the next day, when it will be fit for immediate use. If made according to these directions, it will be a very superior toilet soap.

CHAPTER V.

91.—STAINS ON LINEN AND COTTON.

STAINS are too often a convenient excuse for indifferent washing. Whatever rubbing will not extract the housewife passes with the satisfying belief that it is a stain, the removal of which is an impossibility. The washerwoman, when confronted with an illy cleaned garment, overcomes censure with the triumphant excuse, "That's a stain; it won't come out." Such excuses, however, would little avail an employee of the city laundry. There are no stains, discolorations or dyes, however indelible they may seem, but what some chemical agent will bleach or extract them. Fine articles discolored with stains look as bad as though they were soiled. In reality, a stain is dirt. Anything foreign to the material is dirt, and the article is still soiled unless the stain be removed. The removal of stains is not near so difficult an operation as is generally supposed. The ability to remove any kind of stain is the pride of laundry establishments, and, from every-day practice, their employees acquire great skill in ascertaining the nature of any stain, and then successfully extracting it. A number of methods and expedients are presented in this chapter, and they embrace nearly every variety of stains. Many of the chemical agents used in these methods are probably unfamiliar to most persons; but this fact should never deter them from employing the methods, whenever they may have an occasion for removing stains from valued articles. They are methods in every-day use, and are the most reliable and practical that can be used. The various chemicals may be obtained from any druggist. Wherever any precaution should attend the use of them it is fully stated, and, as far as possible, their chemical action is explained. It is often difficult to determine whether a stain will come out easily or not. Frequently, what appears to be a stain difficult of removal comes out by the simplest method; vice versa, simple stains often require careful treatment. Of course, the simpler the remedy competent to effect the cure, the better. The following stain methods embody not only distinct classes of stains, but methods for general cases are also given. When the origin of the stain is obscure, a general method will be found very useful. Ladies can use their judgment in regard to which method is the most applicable to the particular case they may have for treatment. If one expedient fails, resort to another. Persevering and repeated application will rarely fail.

92.—STAINS PRODUCED BY VEGETABLE JUICES.

FRUIT stains, wine stains, and those produced by colored vegetable juices, are often nearly indelible, and require various treatment. They may always be removed, however, if a little perseverance is exercised. Among the expedients resorted to, the following are the most effectual. Always carefully examine the linen, and extract all stains of this class previous to washing; for the stains are apt to be set so firmly by soap-suds that their removal is rendered exceedingly difficult.

93.—FRUIT STAINS IN LINEN.

TO remove fruit stains in linen, rub each side of the portion stained with yellow soap; then tie up a piece of Pearl-ash in the cloth and soak it well in hot water, or boil it if the stain be obstinate. Afterward, expose the stained part to the action of the air and sun until the stain disappears.

94.—WINE STAINS IN LINEN.

THIS is a simple and generally a very successful method of extracting wine stains: Hold the stained part of the article in milk that is boiling on the stove. Usually this will soon take out the stain, and the process is attended with no injury whatever to the fabric.

95.—SPECIAL AGENTS FOR OBDURATE CASES.

OBDURATE fruit and wine stains of almost any variety may be removed by using some one of the following ingredients: A weak solution of Chlorine Chloride of Lime, Spirits of Salts, Oxalic Acid, or Salts of Lemon, in warm water. Quite frequently, a little Lemon Juice will be sufficient. Each of these ingredients should be diluted with warm water, and the stained part should be well washed with water only, previous to applying them. Let the stained portion lie in the solution about two minutes; after which, the article should be rinsed in warm water, free from soap, and then dried. Stains of this class may sometimes be taken out by soaking the linen in sour Buttermilk, and then drying in the heat of the sun. Afterward, wash in clean cold water. Repeat the process two or three times a day until it is successful.

96.—CLARET AND PORT WINE STAINS.

APPLY some table-salt to the stained spot, and moisten it with a little Sherry. After washing, no trace of the stain will be left. The acid which the Sherry contains decomposes the salt, and Chlorine (Bleaching Gas) is set free, which destroys the vegetable coloring matter of the wine. If it is a port wine stain, the Sherry should be likewise added to the salt, as the port also contains acid.

97.—ACID AND TEA STAINS.

SPIRITS of Hartshorn, diluted with an equal quantity of water, will often remove stains produced by acids, tea, wine or fruits. After the application of the Hartshorn, the article should be well rinsed in cold water. In difficult cases it may be necessary to repeat the application several times before the stains are entirely removed.

98.—OLD FRUIT AND WINE STAINS.

FRUIT and wine stains which have remained for some time, and have become seemingly indelibly set, should be subjected to this treatment: Rub each side of the stain with yellow soap, and then apply very thickly a paste of Starch and cold water. Rub the paste well in, and expose the linen to the action of the sun and air until the stain disappears. As it becomes dry, sprinkle it from time to time with a little water. If not removed in three or four days, rub off the paste and renew the process. A second application rarely fails.

99.—STAINED NAPKINS AND TABLE-CLOTHS.

NAPKINS, table-cloths or other white fabrics that are stained with coffee or fruits, previous to being put into soap-suds, should have boiling water turned over them, and be allowed to soak until the water becomes cold; then rub out the spots in this water. If they are put into soap-suds with the stains in them, the suds will set the stains so that no subsequent washing will remove them. Table-cloths and napkins will be far less likely to become stained if they are always starched a little, as the starch has a tendency to prevent coffee and juices of fruits from penetrating into the texture of the cloth.

100.—PROCESS OF SULPHURATION.

SULPHUROUS Acid Gas is often employed to bleach out stains, and is very effectual. It may be generated at the moment of using by burning a little piece of sulphur under the wide end of a small paper funnel, the upper orifice of which is applied near the stain, which must be previously moistened with hot water.

Coffee and chocolate stains, when every other means fail, may be removed by carefully washing in very hot water, and then subjecting the spot to sulphuration. In the case of slight stains, a lighted sulphur match held under the stain will produce sufficient Sulphurous Acid Gas to bleach out the stain. Stains caused by any vegetable acid can generally be removed by sulphuration.

Sulphuric Acid diluted with water, or water acidulated with a little Muriatic or Oxalic Acid, is very effectual in removing fruit stains. Care must be taken not to have the acidulated water so strong as to eat a hole in the cloth. As soon as the stain is out, rinse in Pearl-ash water, and then through fair water.

101.—TO REMOVE IRON RUST.

STAINS of iron rust are frequently quite obstinate and their removal very difficult to accomplish by the direct application of any reagent. If, however, the nature of the stain be changed, or a new stain be created, the new stain, together with the iron rust, can be readily removed. First, moisten the part stained, with Ink, and then remove the Ink with Muriatic Acid diluted with five or six times its weight of water. In this treatment it will be found that the old and new stains have been simultaneously removed. This is a very effectual method, even in the most difficult cases.

102.—INK SPOTS.

SPOTS of common or indelible ink may be removed by saturating them with Lemon Juice, and then rubbing on common Salt. Afterward, place them where the hot rays of the sun will shine on them for several hours. As fast as they dry, rub on more Lemon Juice and Salt. When Lemon Juice is not easy to obtain, Citric Acid makes a good substitute. Iron rust may sometimes be removed in the same manner. A solution of Chloride of Lime (38) is also largely employed in laundries for removing ink spots. Soaking cotton goods that have common ink spilt on them, in lukewarm sour milk, will frequently be successful.

103.—DELICATE FABRICS STAINED WITH INK OR IRON MOULD.

TO extract ink or iron mould from delicate linen fabrics, wet the spots with Milk and then cover them with common Salt. Then lay them in the heat of the sun, and wet them occasionally as they dry. Another way to take out ink stain is to dip the spot in melted Tallow. This is the best plan to employ for fine, delicate articles.

104.—ESSENTIAL SALTS OF LEMON.

ESSENTIAL Salts of Lemon, so useful in extracting ink, iron rust and many other stains from linen and cotton, is made as follows: Take one ounce of Oxalic Acid in powder and mix it with four ounces of Cream of Tartar. The mixture ought to be preserved in small round boxes. In using, wet the finger with water and dip it in the powder; then gently rub the spot, keeping it rather moist, and the stain will disappear without injury to the fabric. This preparation is not the Lemon Essence used in lemonade making, but, if swallowed, is very poisonous. It should be labeled, *poison*.

105.—IRON RUST AND INK STAINS OF LONG STANDING.

THE removal of these stains is a matter of some difficulty if they have remained long on the fabric. It can be done, however, by applying Oxalic Acid in powder upon the spots, which must be previously moistened with water. After the acid has been well rubbed in, it should be thoroughly washed out; for Oxalic Acid is highly corrosive to textile fabrics. Care should always be exercised in employing strong acids; for they are very apt to injure and rot the cloth.

106.—YELLOW SULPHIDE OF AMMONIA.

THIS method is free from the objections against the use of strong acids, and will remove stains of long standing almost immediately. Wet the marks of ink or iron mould with Yellow Sulphide of Ammonia, by which they will be immediately blackened. Allow it to remain a minute or two for the stains to become well blackened. Then, with water, wash out the excess of Ammonia Sulphide, and treat the remaining black spot with cold dilute Muriatic Acid, whereby it will be immediately removed. Finally, wash well with water.

107.—TO EXTRACT MILDEW.

FROM the nature of mildew stains, it is obvious that their successful removal may be attended with some difficulty. Several methods are here presented. A lady can easily determine which is best adapted to any particular case. If one method fails, try another. In removing mildew and many other stains, a great reliance may be placed upon the bleaching powers of "Old Sol." Rub soap thoroughly on the mildew spots; then scrape some Chalk, and rub that also over the spots. Lay the linen on the grass in the heat of the sun, and its rays will bleach out the spots. As it dries, wet it a little, and the mildew will come out, at the farthest, in the second application.

108.—STARCH AND SALT METHOD.

ANOTHER successful way of removing mildew is to mix together soft Soap, powdered Starch, half as much Salt as Starch, and the juice of a Lemon, and apply the mixture to the spots with a brush. Let the article lay on the grass day and night until the mildew disappears. This recipe is a good one.

109.—CHLORIDE OF LIME.

TAKE two ounces of Chloride of Lime and pour over it a quart of boiling water; then add three quarts of cold water. Steep the mildewed linen in this solution for an hour, when every spot will be extracted. On taking the linen out of the solution, immerse it immediately in boiling water, and let it soak for fifteen minutes (38). Fruit and wine stains may also be removed in this way. Some grades of linen which have contracted mildew may require repeated applications for two or three days, rinsing out and bleaching in the sunshine after each application.

110.—OXALIC AND CITRIC ACID SOLUTION.

A VERY good solution for extracting mildew may be prepared by mixing together Oxalic Acid, Citric

Acid and Milk. Rub it well into the spots; repeat as it dries; thoroughly wash and bleach on the grass. Quite often mildew may be removed by simply dipping the stained portion in sour Buttermilk, laying it in the sunshine, and, as soon as it is white, rinsing in fair water.

111.—STAIN METHOD FOR SUMMER USE.

THE juice of green Tomatoes thickly mixed with Salt will remove stains of various kinds from white goods. The mixture is applied to the stain, and the article then exposed to the action of the sun. During the summer and fall, when articles are most likely to become stained with fruits, &c., this will be found a very practical method, as the ingredients can be readily obtained. It can be used for white goods only, as the Tomato Juice will destroy colors. On account of its simplicity and inability to injure the cloth, it would be advisable to try this method before resorting to others. A great variety of stains, fruit, wine, ink, iron rust, mildew, &c., even when they are quite obstinate, will yield to this treatment.

112.—ACID AND ALKALI STAINS.

IF the discoloration has been produced by acids, Aqua Ammonia will generally remove it. If it has been produced by Alkaline Substances, moderately strong Vinegar should be applied. When the article is delicate, the Vinegar should be discolored by being filtered through powdered Charcoal. Acid stains on linen may also be removed by wetting the part and applying some Salts of Wormwood (Carbonate of Potassa). Then rub the Salts of Wormwood well into the cloth, without diluting it with water. These agents will almost immediately neutralize the stains.

113.—NITRIC ACID STAINS.

WHENEVER nitric acid in any quantity falls on an article, it is apt to burn a hole through the fabric, and, in that case, it would be useless, of course, to try the following method. If the stain be slight and the threads not actually consumed, then the original color may be restored by this method: Apply to the stain a solution of Permanganate of Potassium; then, while the fabric is moist, expose it to the fumes of burning sulphur (100).

114.—MILK STAINS.

IN extracting milk stains, they should be first soaked in Benzoin to remove the fatty portion of the milk;

and afterward in warm Borax Water, as strong as it can be made, and containing Potash in the proportion of half an ounce to a pint of Borax Water. Sometimes old milk stains are very difficult to remove, and require continued applications.

115.—PERSPIRATION STAINS.

THE stains produced by perspiration are not unfrequently quite obstinate. The best way to remove them is to apply a strong solution of Soda. A concentrated Soda solution seldom fails to bleach out the stains. Afterward, the part should be thoroughly rinsed in warm water, to prevent the Soda from injuring the fabric.

116.—TO DISSOLVE OLD BLOOD STAINS.

OLD blood stains that have become set may be dissolved out of the cloth by this treatment: Apply to the stains a solution of Iodide of Potassa in four times its weight of water. The Iodide of Potassa should be then washed out with warm water, and it will be found that the blood stains have entirely disappeared.

117.—TO REMOVE STAINS OF IODINE.

VARIOUS preparations of Iodine are largely employed for medicinal applications, and their use is always dreaded on account of the bad stains they leave. Stains of Iodine may be removed by rectified Spirits; or, what is still better, any Tincture of Iodine may be prevented from leaving a stain after it is used. Add a few drops of liquid Carbolic Acid to the Iodine Tincture, and the latter will leave no stain. A good medical authority recommends Carbolic Acid as rendering the efficacy of Tincture of Iodine more certain.

118.—ANILINE RED (MAGENTA).

STAINS of aniline red may be readily extracted by the application of Cyanide of Potassa. Simply soak the stained portion of the article for a few minutes in a weak solution of Cyanide of Potassa, which will neutralize the stain. The article should be well rinsed immediately after the application. This is a never-failing method.

119.—SOOT STAINS.

STAINS caused by soot, or contracted while handling stove-pipes, are usually not difficult to extract.

In cases where simple means fail, the following method may be successfully employed: First, wash the spot with Sulphuric Acid diluted with water, and then rinse in clear water. Care must be taken to sufficiently dilute the Sulphuric Acid, or else it may injure the cloth.

120.—TAR, PITCH, RESIN, PAINT, ETC.

THIS method includes all cases where the staining substance is of a resinous character: Pour on the spots a little Alcohol, and let it soak in about half an hour. Then rub it gently, and it will be found that the Alcohol has dissolved out the glutinous quality, so that the residue will easily crumble out. Chloroform, also, is an excellent medium to remove paint stains from articles. Portions of dry white paint that have resisted the action of Alcohol, Ether, or Benzoin, are at once removed by Chloroform. Turpentine or Alcohol will answer very well when the stains are fresh.

121.—YELLOW CLAY STAINS.

WHENEVER red shale and certain varieties of clay come in contact with white goods, they leave conspicuous red or yellow stains. In wet weather, the bottom of white skirts are especially liable to become discolored with shale or clay mud. Very often stains of this kind cannot be washed out with soap and water, without rubbing the article nearly to shreds. The best and speediest way of removing such stains is to pass the skirt or discolored article through the Laundry "Bleach" (38). This process will entirely obliterate every trace of the stain, and at the same time give the article a beautiful whiteness.

122.—GREASE SPOTS.

SCOURING drops, which will remove spots of grease from linen or any other material, may be made by mixing together Spirits of Turpentine and Essence of Lemon, of each one ounce. The Essence must be newly made, or it will leave a circle around the spot. This method is applicable not only to linen and cotton, but is also excellent for extracting grease from silks, woolens, or goods of any material.

123.—NON-METALLIC STAINS.

THIS method possesses general powers, and will remove nearly all stains which are not metallic. Mix two tablespoonfuls of water with one of Spirits of

Salts (Muriatic Acid) Let the stained part lie in this mixture for one or two minutes, and then rinse in cold water. This treatment will be found particularly useful in removing stains from white napkins and tablecloths.

124.—SCOURING BALLS FOR GENERAL USE.

IN order to remove a stain the cause or origin of which is doubtful, a composition is requisite which possesses various powers. Egg scouring balls, the formula for preparing which is given below, are excellent for such a purpose: Dissolve a quarter of a pound of white Soap in a glassful of Alcohol, and beat into this the Yolks of four or five Eggs. Add, gradually, a little Spirits of Hartshorn, and then incorporate with the mixture sufficient Fuller's Earth to convert the whole into solid balls. Prepared in this manner, the balls will be always convenient for use. In removing the stain, wet the stained part with soft water, and then rub it with a ball of the above composition, which should be well worked into the cloth. Then thoroughly wash out the composition. Egg scouring balls will remove almost any stain except ink spots and stains caused by various solutions of iron.

125.—STAIN MIXTURES.

SOME laundry establishments always keep on hand stain mixtures for general use. Such mixtures are very valuable in cases where the nature of the stain is not understood. Also, for stains for which there is no special method; or, when a method which seems to be particularly adapted to certain cases fails to remove the stain, then a general stain mixture can be advantageously employed. Two of the best stain mixtures for general use are given below:

MIXTURE No. 1.—Dissolve half an ounce of Sorrel in half a pint of water, and add two ounces of Spirits of Wine. Shake them all well together. Apply the mixture to the stain with a sponge.

MIXTURE No. 2.—Mix together an ounce each of Sal Ammonia and Salts of Tartar, and add one pint of soft water.

126.—TO RESTORE SCORCHED LINEN.

ALTHOUGH appearing an impossibility, yet even where articles are badly scorched, the color can be restored. The composition used for this purpose will doubtless seem to be prepared from singular ingredients; but experience has proved that it will successfully accomplish the desired result. It is hardly necessary to state that it is needless to apply the composition if the texture of the linen is so much burnt that no strength is left. Nothing, in that case, could prevent a hole from being formed, although the composition by no means tends to injure the fabric. If, however, the scorching is not quite through and the threads not actually consumed, then the application of the composition, followed by two or three good washings, will restore the linen to its original color. The marks of the scorching will be totally effaced, and the place will seem as white and perfect as any other part of the linen. Mix well together two ounces of Fuller's Earth reduced to powder, one ounce of Bird Guano, half an ounce of cake Soap finely scraped, and the juice of two large onions. The onions should be sliced, beaten in a mortar, and pressed. Boil this mass in half a pint of strong Vinegar, stirring it from time to time, till it forms a thick liquid compound. Spread this composition thickly over the scorched part, and let it remain for twenty-four hours. If the scorching was light, one application, with the assistance of two subsequent washings, will be sufficient to restore the whiteness. If, however, the scorching was strong, a second coating should be given after the removal of the first, and this likewise allowed to remain for twenty-four hours. After the linen has been washed two or three times, and the scorching is still visible, apply the composition again, and a complete cure will seldom fail to be effected. It rarely ever happens that a third application is necessary. The remainder of the composition may be kept for future use by preserving it in a gallipot, covered and tied over with bladder.

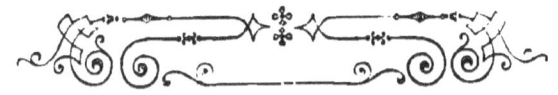

CHAPTER VI.

127.—CARE OF LINEN.

IT is an excellent plan and consistent with economy, to carefully examine and repair all articles which require it, previous to consigning them to the laundry. Much after work is often thus saved. It is also prudent to number articles, and so arrange them after they are washed, that they may have their regular turn and term in domestic use. When linen is well dried, aired, and laid away for use, nothing further is necessary, except to secure it from damp and insects.

128.—AROMATIC HERBS.

AN agreeable way to protect linen from insects, is to intersperse among the drawers and shelves a judicious mixture of aromatic shrubs and flowers, cut up and sewed in silken bags. The mixture may coneist of Lavender, Thyme, Roses, Cedar Shavings, powdered Sassafras, Cassia, Lignia, &c., to which may be added a few drops of Attar of Roses, or other strong scented perfume.

129.—LAVENDER SCENT BAG.

THE drawers and linen may be nicely perfumed, by a Lavender Scent Bag, which can be made as follows: Take half a pound of Lavender Flowers, free from stalks; half an ounce each of dried Thyme and Mint, a quarter of an ounce each of ground Cloves and Carraway, and one ounce of common Salt, dried. Mix the whole well together, and sew up the product in silk or cambric bags.

130.—TO KEEP AWAY MOTHS, BEETLES, ETC.

SEW up a piece of Camphor in a linen bag, and place a few of these bags in the drawers, among the linen and woolen goods, and neither moth nor worm will come near them. Brimstone, in rolls, put away with articles, will prevent moths, and no odor is imparted to the clothes.

131.—AN AGREEABLE PERFUME.

A VERY pleasant perfume, and also a preventive against moths, may be made of the following ingredients: Take one ounce each, of Cloves, Carraway Seeds, Nutmeg, Mace, Cinnamon, and Tonquin Beans, and then add as much Florentine Orris Root as will equal the other ingredients put together. Grind the whole well together, and then sew it in little bags, and place them among the clothes.

132.—A DELICATE PERFUME FOR KID GLOVES.

THE following, is an excellent perfume for kid gloves, ribbons, laces, &c. Take one drachm each of Ambergris and Civet, and add a quarter of an ounce of Flour-Butter. Mix them all well together. Rub the gloves over gently with the perfume, applying it with fine cotton wool, and press the perfume into them (264.)

133.—LAYING AWAY SUMMER GOODS.

IT is customary with many ladies, to wash, starch and iron summer clothing when laying it away for the winter. The goods are laundried just as if they were to be worn in a day or two. This is very bad policy; for starched articles, when laid away for months, without use, are extremely liable to turn yellow and mildew. In such cases, the best way is to simply "rough-dry" them, that is, wash and strongly blue them, but do not starch or even iron them, and roll them up for laying away, instead of folding. Lace curtains, and all delicate summer goods, when laid away "rough-dried," will be found uninjured when wanted again.

134.—INDELIBLE INK.

IT is obvious, that in a well regulated family, every article should be marked with the owner's name or initial, and carefully numbered. Trouble is often had in obtaining a good indelible ink for marking clothes. Many marking inks, although black when first applied to the linen, become gradually washed out, and a yellowish stain only remains. A good indelible ink should have the following properties:

It should flow freely from the pen, without running or blotting.

It should not require very strong or long-continued heat to develop the required hue. Merely passing a hot iron over the marks, or by holding the cloth to the fire, should bring out a perfectly black mark.

It should not injure the texture of the finest fabric.

A recipe is given below for an indelible ink, from the formula of Jules Guiller, a celebrated chemist. This ink can be easily made, and answers all the above requisites.

135.—FORMULA FOR MAKING INDELIBLE INK

Nitrate of Silver,	5 drachms,
Distilled water,	12 "
Powdered Gum-Arabic,	5 "
Carbonate of Soda,	7 "
Ammonia,	10 "

Dissolve the Carbonate of Soda in the Distilled Water, and diffuse through the solution the powdered Gum-Arabic. Dissolve the Nitrate of Silver in the Ammonia, and commingle this with the other solution. Next, warm the mixed fluids in a flask, by which they become at first grayish black and partly coagulated, subsequently brown and clear; then, when ebullition begins, very dark, and of such a consistency that the ink flows readily from a pen. No precipitate forms in this ink; and by boiling, its color becomes darker. Prepared in the above manner, it produces very black marks upon linen. It can be used with a clean steel pen, and is also very suitable for marking with stamps or stencil plates.

136.—SURE METHOD OF DISINFECTING.

A KNOWLEDGE of some simple and effectual method for disinfecting wearing apparel, bed clothes, or other fabrics, which have become infected with contagious matter, is not unfrequently of great importance. Where not only the dreaded small-pox and yellow fever, but even the more common contagious diseases, scarlatina, measels, typhus and malarial fevers prevail, articles in the sick room and about the person of the patient quickly become infected with the poison and readily spread the disease. In all such cases, disinfection should be thorough before the articles are put to further use; and the knowledge of the best method for accomplishing this purpose will be of great value. The precaution may prevent the sickness or death of loved ones.

During the terrible yellow fever epidemic of '78, when the merciless scourge swept over the sunny South, nearly depopulating the beautiful valley of the Mississippi, it became the duty of the Post Office and Treasury Departments at Washington, to adopt the surest method possible for disinfecting mail matter, money packages, and all articles coming from the infected cities. The protection of the government clerks, upon whom devolved the handling of such matter, demanded that the method should be absolutely certain. After elaborate experiments, the disinfecting agent selected was Gasoline. It was found that when letters, money packages, or packages of linen, cotton, woolen, or silk goods were saturated with Gasoline, the liquid evaporated almost immediately, leaving the article thoroughly disinfected, and without the slightest injury to the color or texture of the finest fabric. This was an important discovery, as Gasoline is undoubtedly the surest and best disinfectant for such a purpose. In all cases where it is necessary to disinfect articles impregnated with contagious poison, immerse them in Gasoline; or, where immersion is impracticable, sponge the surface with Gasoline. In less than five minutes, the liquid will evaporate, leaving not the slightest trace of its presence, and the disinfection will be effectual.

137.—TO RENDER GARMENTS FIRE-PROOF.

TO render garments fire-proof is a very simple operation, and, in certain cases, a knowledge of the process may be of advantage. A solution containing five per cent. of Phosphate of Ammonia will render dress goods, into which it is rubbed, perfectly fire-roof. Thoroughly saturate the goods with the solution, and dry them away from the fire. Even if gunpowder is exploded on goods thus treated, they will only char, not blaze.

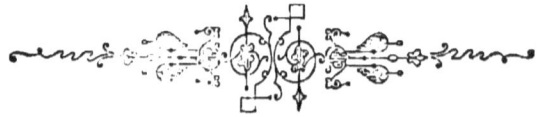

CHAPTER VII.

138.—IMPROVED METHOD OF CUTTING AND MAKING SHIRTS.

PERHAPS a treatise on shirt manufacture may appear to be beyond the limits of a Laundry Guide; yet the art of neatly laundrying and glossing shirts has been presented so explicitly that it seems a pity to bestow such labor upon an illy-fitting garment. However beautifully done up a shirt may be, the effect is vastly impaired if an accurate fit be not possessed. How often on Sabbath mornings, while the clean linen is being donned, is the serenity of the day broken and the wife or mother made uncomfortable by impatient fault-findings. Every lady, the happy possessor of a husband or son particular and difficult to please, is familiar with such a scene. An uncomfortable fitting shirt is, in truth, perfectly abominable to the wearer; and gentlemen are so proverbially fault-finding in this respect that we present to ladies this chapter on Improved Shirt Cutting and Making, with the confidence that it will be highly acceptable.

It is well understood that both the quality and durability of the shirt of home manufacture are far superior to those of custom make, and it is no more labor to have the home-made shirt of a correct fit than of an imperfect one. The trouble of cutting is the same, and no more stitches need be taken. Nor is there any particular skill demanded in acquiring this art, so little understood, of neatly fitting a shirt: all that is needed is some plan whereby exact measurements may be taken and applied, in consequence of which the fit of the shirt will be accurate. Former charts and designs for cutting shirt patterns have been so vague and difficult to comprehend that they are of little value. They perplex rather than aid the maker. The method here presented was taught us by a professional shirt-maker, one who has the reputation of making a shirt fit as neatly as a glove. This method is so natural and easy to understand, and, withal, so reliable, that any lady, who never in her life made a shirt, can, by its aid, readily cut and make one, either for the smallest boy or the largest man, that will set admirably. Surely, the satisfaction and pleasure which such a shirt affords, both to the wearer and maker, is of no small enjoyment.

139.—SELECTION OF MATERIAL.

IT will always be found the most economical in the long run to procure the best brand of muslin out of which to make the shirt. Every one, of course, has their preference. Very thick, heavy muslin, however, although it may be of excellent quality, is not the best for this purpose. It is hard to wash and iron, and in wearing is apt to crack and break. Some fine brand of light weight is preferable, and the shirt made of such quality of muslin will last much longer.

140.—SHRINKING THE MUSLIN.

BEFORE cutting the material, it should always be shrunk. This can be well done by washing the muslin in warm soap-suds, and then hanging it in a position where the hot rays of the sun will quickly dry it. This process will prevent many familiar complaints of shirts becoming too small, or of the linen in the bosom and cuffs getting looser than the lining, faults so common in the shirts of manufactories.

141.—COMMON FAULTS IN THE FIT OF A SHIRT.

THE principal parts of a shirt are, the body, yoke, sleeves, and the bosom; besides these, there are several minor parts—collar, cuffs, bands, gussets, and tongue. By observing the wrinkles which form in a shirt during a day's wear, faults in its fit may be readily ascertained. The most common are, that it is not cut out enough in the neck, is too long on the shoulder, and across the chest is too broad. The first of these faults causes the bosom to bulge. By the two latter, wrinkles and creases are formed around the arms. These faults may be easily guarded against, if the proper measurements be taken.

142.—SEVEN MEASUREMENTS.

A GOOD fitting shirt requires seven measurements, and these measurements cannot be taken with too great accuracy. They are as follows:

First.—The length of the garment. This measurement is taken from the nape of the neck downward, and may be longer or shorter at will, preference varying in regard to the length of the shirt.

Second.—The breadth of the chest from one arm to the other.

Third.—The length of the bosom. For this, two measurements are required. The first, directly in front, from the base of the neck to the waist. The second, from the top of the shoulder, where it joins the neck, to a corresponding point of the waist.

Fourth.—The length of the shoulder. This is taken from the point where the shoulder joins the neck to the tip or extremity of the shoulder.

Fifth.—The size around the neck. This should be taken in the smallest part of the neck, allowing one inch over the measurement. Mark this in full, and also mark one-third of it.

Sixth.—The length of the sleeve. Measure down the inside of the arm, and allow two inches more for the length on the outside.

Seventh.—The size of the wrist, taken loosely.

143.—DIMENSIONS OF A SHIRT OF MEDIUM SIZE.

NOW, in order to give these measurements more clearness, the dimensions of a medium-size shirt will be assumed. Suppose the length of the prospective shirt to be a yard and an eighth; the length of the sleeve five-eighths of a yard, and three-eighths sufficient for yoke, bands, &c. Three and a fourth yards of material, seven-eighths in width, will accordingly be required. From this quantity cut off what is to be used for sleeves, yoke, &c., and there is left for the body two and a fourth yards, twice the assumed length, since the shirt is made of two breadths. Double the two and a fourth yards in the width, and cut apart—one breadth being for the back, the other for the front.

144.—THE MODERN SHIRT—FRONT BREADTH.

THE front breadth of the modern-styled shirt, having a shield-shape bosom, is now prepared as follows: Fold the muslin in the length, having the edges at the top and bottom exactly even. First, take the second measurement (142), which is from one arm to the other across the chest, or from A to B, Plate I. The more exactness with which this measurement is taken, the neater the front of the shirt will fit. This is one of the most important points. Having the muslin folded, only one-half of the measurement across the chest is needed. Mark this, and let it remain until the third measurement is taken, which, as before stated, consists of two—the first, directly in front, from the

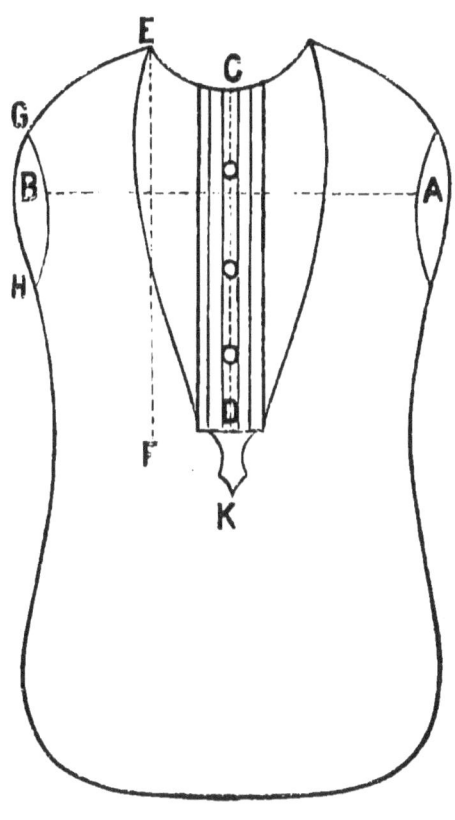

PLATE I.

MODERN SHIRT—FRONT BREADTH.

base of the neck, C, to the waist, D; the second, from the shoulder at the neck, E, to a corresponding point, F, of the waist. Now, hollow from the base of the neck, C, to the shoulder, E. By hollowing in this manner, a sure fit at the neck will be gained, and the bosom can never bulge or wrinkle.

145.—SHOULDER MEASUREMENT.

NEXT, obtain the shoulder measurement. Measure from the point, E, Plate I, where the shoulder joins the neck, to the tip of the shoulder, G. This should be carefully taken; for no shirt will set well if it be too long on the shoulder. Now, cut the armhole from the tip of the shoulder, G, to the point, B, of the chest measure, by hollowing gradually until cut in to the point, B. As this is but half of the front of the armhole, hollow the other half outward until the point, H, under the arm, is reached, two inches farther out than the point, B. Shape the body of the shirt by hollowing it as represented in Plate I. The front breadth of the shirt is now cut, and is ready for the bosom.

146.—THE SHIELD BOSOM.

THE bosom may be home-made or bought ready-made, at will, and may be of any style of plaits fancied. It should always be lined with heavy white drilling, or, if muslin be used, with three folds. The drilling, however, is always the best. The bosom should be set on over the muslin of the shirt, leaving the muslin for an extra lining. Too great pains cannot be taken to have the bosom well lined; for it protects the linen from cracking or breaking, the linen can be starched stiffer, and a finer gloss may be imparted. Care must also be taken to set the bosom on straight. This object is easily attained by creasing the bosom lengthwise in the centre, likewise the front of the shirt, and then basting in the bosom, placing crease to crease. The bosom should be stitched on with a double row of stitching, about half an inch apart. It is customary to attach to the base of the bosom, in the centre, a pointed bit of cloth, double—the tongue, K, Plate I - which is provided with a buttonhole, corresponding to the button in the waistband of the drawers, and is designed to keep the shirt bosom well in its place when worn. Stitch a small band on the edge of the bosom to conceal the edge. Finish the bottom of the breadth with a small hem, and then three small eyelets worked in the bosom completes the front breadth.

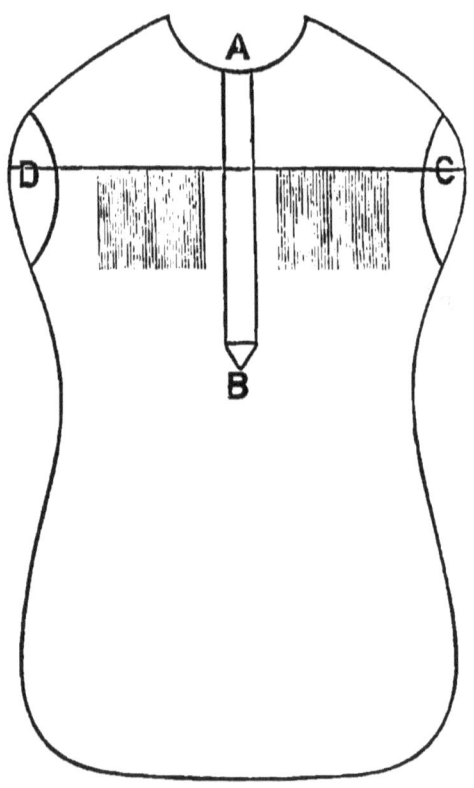

PLATE II.
BACK BREADTH.

147.—BACK BREADTH—PLATE II.

THE back breadth will now be considered. Fold this breadth lenthwise in the centre, and cut the back opening, A to B, about eight or ten inches in length. To prevent the shirt from gaping at the back, lay a wide hem on the left side. In this hem the buttonholes are worked. Face the other side of the opening with a strip of muslin about an inch wide, and sew the buttons on this facing, which is much better than a hem for firmly holding the buttons. Lay the hem over upon the facing, and fasten them together, with a double row of stitching, at the bottom.

Previous to shaping the armholes of the back, it is always best to sew on the yoke. Gather the back on each side. Lay the gathers neatly, making the gathered spaces correspond on each side, and fasten with thread. The back breadth is now ready for the yoke.

148.—THE YOKE.

THE yoke is cut as in Plate III, which represents one-half of it, laying as it should be cut upon the material. For an exact fit of the yoke, take its measurement across the back from one shoulder to the other, from C to D, Plate II. Only one-half of this measurement is required, as the yoke is cut in four pieces, two pieces being for the lining. Make the shoulder of the yoke, A—B, Plate III, the same length as the shoulder of the front breadth (145). In depth, the yoke may be of any length desired. Hollow the neck a little from A to C. Cut in this manner, the yoke will have an excellent fit.

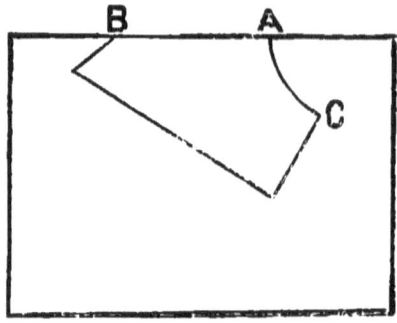

PLATE III.
HALF OF YOKE.

149.—JOINING THE BREADTHS.

NOW sew the shoulder of the two breadths together, and hollow the armholes of the back to correspond with those of the front. The armholes of the back, however, need not be hollowed so deep as those of the front; for the fit of the shirt is not at all affected whether the back be cut narrow or wide. Shape the body of the back under the arms as represented in Plate II. Finish the yoke with buttons and buttonholes. Now seam up the sides, leaving them open about four inches at the bottom. It will be found useful to put in small gussets at the points where the side seams begin to be open.

150.—NECK BAND.

AS the neck has been already cut out, ascertain if it be correct by applying the neck measurement, which was taken the exact size of the neck in the smallest part, and an inch over the measurement allowed. The neck is now finished with the binding, made to be about an inch wide, and upon which are sewed the buttons to hold the collar in place. After being doubled, the binding should be hollowed in front to a half-inch, the hollow beginning at a point corresponding to the point where the hollowed part of the bosom begins. Run the cut parts in a small seam on the wrong side, turn the band on the right side and stitch it on the upper edge. After this has been done, the band is basted on the shirt and stitched. The body of the shirt is now finished. In taking the foregoing measurements and applying them, the Plates representing each piece will be found of great assistance.

151.—SLEEVES.

THE sleeves are cut in the manner following: Lay upon the lap-board or work-table the five-eighths

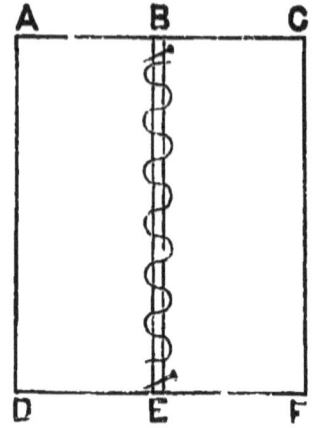

PLATE IV.

FOLDING OF SLEEVE.

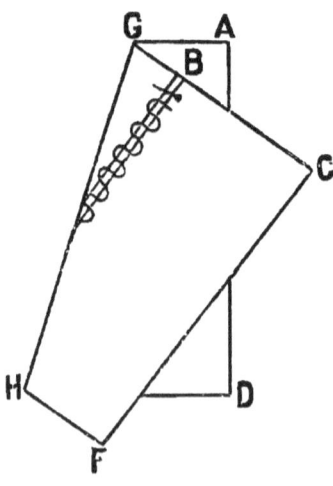

PLATE V.

FOLDING OF SLEEVE.

of a yard of material reserved for this purpose, and fold over each side to meet in the centre, the material being folded in such a manner that the cut edges will be represented by the letters A, B, C and D, E, F, Plate IV, and the selvages meet in the line B, E. The two sleeves, each five-eighths in length and one-half of the width of the material in breadth, are now lying upon the work-table, but not cut apart, and the first care is to unite them still more by basting together the two selvages and securing that seam well in its place, as represented in Plate IV, by pins at the top and bottom. Thus prepared, fold it diagonally, as represented in Plate V, the selvages meeting from the point, B, downward. Cut from G to H, and sew together each portion of the basted selvages. The sleeves, each with its gore, are now ready. Before being sewed up, however, they should be gathered at the lower edge, and about an inch left plain at each end near the opening. This opening at the bottom of the sleeve should be about three inches in length. Face its upper side with a strip of muslin about an inch wide, pointed at the top and stitched on both sides. Face the other side in a like manner. The sleeve will thus have a nice finish.

152.—CUFFS.

NEXT in order are the cuffs. The measurement of the wrist is taken loosely, and the cuff is cut about four inches in depth, and rounded at the corners. It should be composed of linen and lined with two folds of heavy white drilling (146). Seam the linen and lining together on the wrong side; then turn on the right, and finish around the edge with two rows of stitching. Baste the cuff on the sleeve, sewing the gathers down on the inside and basting the linen on the top, and the whole will then be ready for stitching.

153.—INSERTING THE SLEEVES.

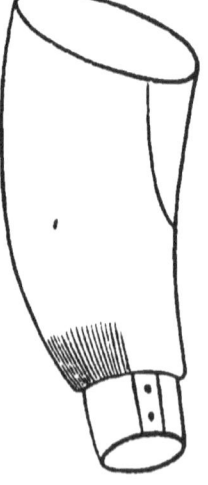

PLATE VI.
SLEEVE FINISHED.

THE bottom of the sleeve being thus finished, sew up the sleeve and prepare the top. Usually the top of the sleeve should be about the same size as the armhole into which it is to be fitted. It may be larger, and then gathered a little on the top, which plan is preferred by some. On no account, however, should it be smaller. In basting in the sleeve, place its seam upon the seam of the shirt, bringing the gore on the back. Stitch the sleeve in with a wide hem, and stitch it down a second time. If the sleeve be too short, a facing

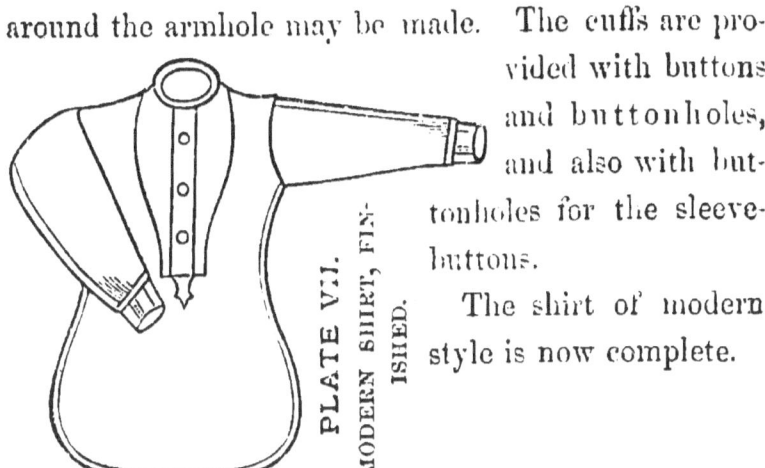

PLATE VII.
MODERN SHIRT, FINISHED.

around the armhole may be made. The cuffs are provided with buttons and buttonholes, and also with buttonholes for the sleeve-buttons.

The shirt of modern style is now complete.

154.—SHIRTS OPENING IN FRONT.

ALTHOUGH the modern shirt with shield-shape bosom, will wear a much longer time without becoming wrinkled, and is far easier to iron and gloss, it is not liked, however, by some gentlemen. Elderly gentlemen, especially, and working men, prefer the old style, with the bosom opening in front. For such, designs are also given. The plan of cutting and making a working shirt, the bosom of which is usually made of the same material as the rest of the shirt, will be first considered, as the same plan, with slight variations, is applicable to the fine shirt of an elderly gentleman, the cutting and making of which can be afterward more readily explained. In the description of both these styles of shirts, many of the details of shirt-making are omitted, for the reason that they have been so fully presented in the consideration of the modern shirt that repetition is useless. In all cases of perplexity, therefore, a lady is referred to the first part of the present chapter. Only the points of difference are given in the styles following.

155.—WORKING SHIRT.

A WORKING shirt may be made of either coarse or fine material, and the measurements required are the same as those for the modern shirt (142). Double the material and cut the two breadths apart. First, prepare the front breadth by beginning with the bosom. For this purpose, cut a slit, A B, Plate VIII, down directly in the middle, beginning at the top of the breadth and making the slit the length indicated by the second measurement of the bosom (142). From the bottom of the slit, then cut across on each side the transverse slits, B C and B D, leaving uncut on the outside a space of six or eight inches. The edges of the slit, A B, are now to be turned down and hemmed, the hem being about an inch in width. On the hem of the right side the buttons will later be sewed, while in that of the left, E, which is to be stitched as indicated by the dotted lines, the buttonholes will be worked. Then make two or three plaits at each side

129

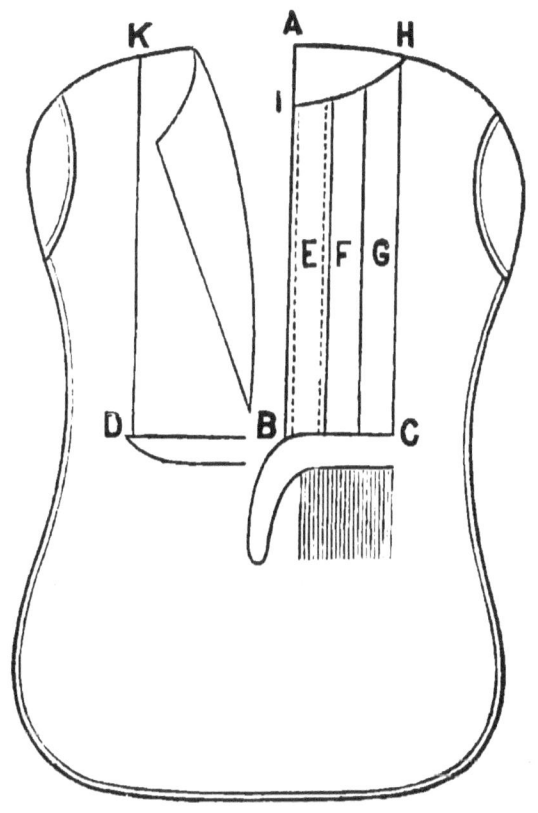

PLATE VIII.

FRONT BREADTH.

of the hem, and hold them in their place by basting threads at the top and bottom. The plaits are represented in Plate VIII by the letters F and G on the left side, the right half being left in course of preparation in order that the explanation may be clearer. After the plaits are thus prepared on both sides, lay the hems evenly one over the other, and secure them in this position, with pins or with stitches at the top and bottom, until the neck has been hollowed out. This last cannot be done until the back and front breadths have been joined together. Now, gather the lower edge of the transverse slit, C D, laying and fastening the gathers so as to make the gathered space of the same length as the breadth of the shirt bosom. Two little strips about an inch wide are next prepared to cover the gathering. Turn over the edges of each strip, and baste one strip upon the outside of the shirt, half upon the bosom and half upon the gathering. Secure this band in its place by a row of stitches across each edge. The other strip is then basted on the wrong side of the shirt in a corresponding position, and hemmed down all around. The lower edge of the breadth is finished with a narrow hem.

156.—BACK BREADTH.

THE back breadth is next prepared. First, gather the upper edge, A to B, Plate IX, straight across,

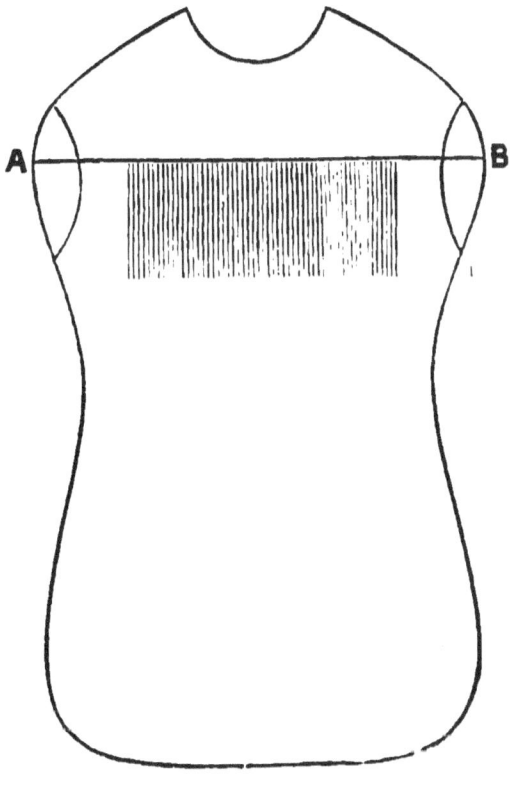

PLATE IX.

BACK BREADTH.

leaving six or eight inches plain on each side. Then lay the gathers and fasten them, making the gathered space to correspond with the width of the shirt bosom. Hem the lower edge of the breadth to match the front. Now, prepare the yoke.

157.—THE YOKE.

THE yoke of the working shirt is put on above the gathers at the back, and is cut by the same measurement and on the same plan as the yoke of the modern shirt. In Plate III (148), half of the yoke is represented laying upon the material as it should be cut. For this yoke four pieces just alike are required, and they should be seamed in the centre. The yoke, however, is much preferable made whole. In that case, double the material before cutting, and thus the seam in the centre will be avoided. Baste the yoke upon the gathers, and stitch them together.

158.—JOINING THE BREADTHS.

THE two breadths of the shirt are now ready to be joined together, which is done by basting the shoulder of the yoke, from the neck to the shoulder tip, upon similar parts of the front. After shaping the body of the breadths as represented in Plates VIII and IX, fell up under the arms, leaving an opening at the bottom about four inches in length. When the two breadths of the shirt are thus joined together, hollow the garment out in the neck from I, the base of the neck, to H, Plate VIII, the point where the shoulder joins the neck — the points I and H being given by the two measurements of the bosom (142). The neck is now ready for the binding, as it has already been cut out in the back. Finish the band with buttons and buttonholes. Prepare the sleeves as in (151), and the working shirt will be completed.

159.—ELDERLY GENTLEMAN'S SHIRT.

IN the working shirt, the garment has been considered made of the same material throughout, but in the case of fine shirts opening in front, the bosom and cuffs are usually made of linen or percale, whichever may be fancied. With the exception of variations in inserting the bosom, the elderly gentleman's shirt is cut and made, in all respects, similar to the working shirt. The bosom is inserted as follows:

160.—THE BOSOM.

HAVING cut the required length, A to B, Plate VIII, remove the whole portion, H, C, D, K, which, in the working shirt, was made into plaits, and use instead a length of linen or percale equal to the length cut away. Retain the whole breadth of the linen to use, if needed, in forming the plaits. This breadth, divided in the centre, gives the two halves of the bosom. The hems and plaits are formed in a manner similar to those of the working shirt, and the two halves are then stitched in their proper places, the stitching beginning at the top at each side. It is more desirable to line the bosom, as any bosom will always last longer, better retain the starch, and is susceptible of a finer gloss, if well lined. In the case of lining the bosom, cut the front breadth similar to the front of the working shirt (155). Cut the front down in the centre the same length as the bosom; baste on the bosom, letting the muslin of the shirt serve as an extra lining, and then stitch the bosom on with a double row of stitching. The under lining may be left loose or caught to the plaits, at will. Finish the shirt in the same manner as the working shirt.

161.—TO STRENGTHEN THE BOSOM.

TO strengthen the bosom in the part most likely to wear, it is a good plan to put a false hem underneath the left hand hem, and in this false hem to work the buttonholes. It must, of course, be a little narrower, so as to be entirely out of sight when the garment is worn. If preferred, the hem of the shirt itself may be a little narrower and receive the buttonholes. A strip of muslin stitched on the outside wholly conceals it, and represents the hem. In either case, any repairs of the buttonholes are concealed, or the whole strip may be removed with but little trouble.

162.—COLLARS.

FOR further instruction in the art of shirt-making, the construction of the collar will now be explained. Originally, the collar was a part of the shirt itself; but, of late years, it has assumed an independent existence. It would appear, judging from the ever-increasing variety of new names applied to this article, that the varieties of collars must be endless. All may be reduced, however, to three original types, the many varieties being simply differences of height, or of the contour of the edge. These three styles are: the standing collar, the turn-down collar, and the collar divided in the back.

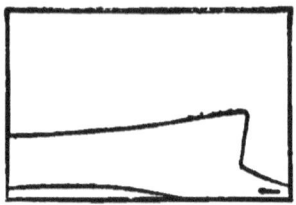

PLATE X.

STANDING COLLARS.

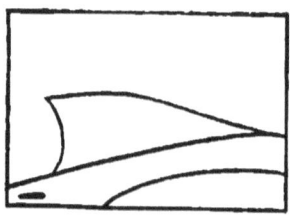

PLATE XI.

TURN-DOWN COLLAR.

163.—CONSTRUCTION OF COLLARS.

ALL collars should be made four-ply, as, by this means, they retain stiffness much longer, and can be more elegantly laundried. In all of the many varieties, a binding is required, which should be cut a little longer than the neck band of the shirt, and be provided with buttonholes corresponding to the buttons on the neck band. For this binding, prepare two strips about an inch wide, and cut them sloping towards the extremities. The collar proper should also be hollowed out a little, as represented in Plates X and XI, somewhat more for a turn-down than for a standing collar. The collar divided in the back is cut in four pieces, and put together so that one-half overlaps the other.

Cuffs of every size and shape are also made separate from the shirt. In this case the wrist band should be made two inches wide, and the cuffs should be provided with buttonholes for the sleeve-buttons, and with additional buttonholes by which to attach them to the buttons of the wrist band.

THE CHEMICAL
LAUNDRY GUIDE.

PART II.

CHAPTER VIII.

164.—PRINTED GOODS OF DELICATE COLORS.

NO dress is more becoming to a lady than the bright and glossy print or percale, when it is new. The soft shades and delicate colors are charming. In how short a time, however, is the lustre gone and the dress faded and dingy through careless washing.

The methods by which the gloss and bright colors of any material may be preserved are easy to follow. To be sure, more time and attention will be required than the usual slight that is given this class of goods, but the result will more than compensate for the extra labor. As well might a lady hope for "good luck" with a cocoanut cake baked in the unwashed pan in which onions have been cooked, as to expect delicate prints to look nice washed in the dirty water through which the general washing has passed.

The best way is not to do up articles of delicate color on the day of the general washing, but to give them a morning by themselves. Undertake them only in clear, bright weather.

The methods presented in this chapter are applicable to colored goods of various materials—percales, piques, chintzes, cambrics, merinoes, prints, lamas, mousse-delaines, ginghams, lawns, printed muslins, alpacas, bombazines, bombazets, book muslins, &c.

In the methods presented for the treatment of various colored goods, it is supposed that the articles are delicate and of some value. It would be needless, of course, to take such pains with old and dingy calicoes. In doing up new and choice goods, however, it will certainly pay to preserve the new appearance and bright colors.

165.—GENERAL HINTS FOR WASHING COLORED GOODS.

COLORED articles before they are put into water should have every grease spot extracted, as the spots cannot be very well seen when the whole of the garment is wet.

No soap is necessary for calicoes, unless they are very dirty. In that case make a strong milk-warm lather and immerse the article in it, instead of rubbing soap on the material.

Soft soap should never be used for printed goods, except the various shades of yellow, which look the best washed with soft soap and not rinsed in fair water. Other colors should be rinsed in fair water.

Never wash colored articles in hot soap-suds; that which is milky-warm will answer quite as well, and will not extract the colors so much.

Never boil or scald colored goods, nor allow them to freeze, as the colors will be irreparably injured.

Always dry this class of goods in the shade, or, if the weather be wet, dry them by the fire. The best prints will fade if hung in the sunshine.

Colored articles should not be allowed to lie in water long, but should be washed fast, always using as much expedition as possible.

166.—GENERAL HINTS FOR IRONING COLORED GOODS.

A GREAT deal of care is often taken in washing goods of delicate colors, but their color and appearance afterward are injured by careless ironing. If the following hints be always observed, the injury in ironing will be avoided:

As soon as they are dry enough, iron them immediately. Do not allow them to lie damp over night, nor sprinkle them. These precautions will protect the goods from getting spotted.

Do not smooth them with a hot sad-iron. Pink and green colors, although they may withstand the washing, are quite liable to change as soon as a hot iron is applied to them, the pink turning purple, and the green blue.

Usually it is best to iron on the wrong side, but, if it be desirable to iron on the right side, use an iron only moderately warm. An excellent plan is to place a piece of muslin between the material and the iron.

167.—TO SET VARIOUS COLORS.

ONE of the chief difficulties to be overcome in washing fine colored articles is the tendency of the colors to mix or run together. The permanence of almost any colored fabric — silk, woolen, or cotton — may be preserved in washing by previously soaking them for some time in water, to every gallon of which has been added a teaspoonful of Ox Gall. This will effectually keep the colors from running. Colors are also preserved by washing the goods in luke-warm Ox Gall water, in the proportion of a teacupful of Gall to four gallons of water. The Gall should be well mixed with the water.

168.—TO PRESERVE OX GALL.

IT is a good policy to have a bottle of Beef or Ox Gall constantly in the house. It is so often convenient, and can be bought of the butchers at a trifle. It may be kept for several months by pressing it out of the skin in which it is enclosed, adding Salt to it, and preserving it in bottles, tightly corked. Ox Gall is a delicate and excellent cleansing agent. It is a liquid soda soap. It is not so good, however, for the purity of white articles, as it has a greenish tinge.

169.—AGENTS FOR SPECIAL COLORS.

THE following substances are remarkably successful for preserving special colors, and should always be used whenever such colors are washed.

A teacupful of Lye in a pailful of water, will improve the color of blacks when it is necessary to wash them.

A spoonful of clear Vinegar in the rinsing water of pink, red, or green colors, will brighten and keep them from mixing. Soda answers the same purpose for purples and blues.

The "Broke-Water" of (51,) is excellent for brightening mixed colors and keeping them from running.

170.—TO RENDER THE COLORS OF NEW GOODS PERMANENT.

IF new goods, before they are ever washed, are subjected to the treatment afforded by this method, their colors will be permanently set, and but little attention need be given them in the future. Dissolve three gills of Salt in four quarts of boiling water. Put the new goods in the solution while it is hot, and let them remain until it becomes cold. By this means, their colors will be rendered permanent, and will be less likely to fade in subsequent washings.

171.—WASHING GOODS OF DELICATE COLORS.

COLORED articles of various materials, printed calicoes, cambrics, chintzes, ginghams, merinoes, alpacas, mousse-de-laines, lamas, bombazines, percales, piques, &c., require nearly the same method in washing, and are treated as follows:

Turn the inner side of the dresses out. Use water that is only luke-warm, and make a strong lather of white soap before putting in the dresses, but do not allow soap itself to come in contact with the material. Wash them through successive lathers, until the last lather does not have a dirty appearance. Do not allow them to remain long in the water, but wash them as fast as possible; and then rinse quickly through two clear cold waters. Dry in the shade. Have the sad-irons ready heated, and while the articles are still a little damp, or just dry enough to iron, bring them in and iron at once. Never sprinkle and roll them in coverings till next day. If it is not convenient to iron immediately, let them hang till quite dry, then on the following day, slightly moisten and fold them a quarter of an hour before ironing. Either iron them on the wrong side, or place a piece of muslin between the goods and the iron. In this method the directions are general and apply to any colored material, but nothing has been said about setting the colors and keeping them from running. For this purpose various colors require different ingredients, both in the washing and rinsing waters, and the subject is fully considered in methods (167) and (169.) If a slip be obtained from the store for testing the durability of its colors, give it a fair trial by this method.

172.—ORIENTAL METHOD OF WASHING BRIGHT COLORS.

IN the countries of the East very dashing and bright colors are in vogue, and Americans are indebted to the Oriental ladies for this skillful method of doing up bright colors. Its chief advantage is, that no soap is used, and the lustre of the goods as well as the color is preserved.

Boil two pounds of Rice in two gallons of water for three hours, or until the Rice becomes soft. After which, pour the whole into a tub and let it stand to cool until about luke-warm. Then place in the articles and wash them till the dirt appears to be out, using the Rice in place of soap. Next make another preparation of Rice and water in the same quantity as above, but this time, strain the Rice from the water. Save the strained water to rinse with, and mix the pulp with warm water. Wash the goods through the latter till quite clean, and then rinse them in the water in which the Rice was boiled. This rinse water answers in place of starch, and the articles will keep nicely stiff when they are worn. Even dew will not affect them. A dress should be taken apart and hung as smoothly as possible to dry. When dry, do not use an iron, as it is liable to scorch; but rub it with a smooth, round, glass bottle, filled with hot water. It is the best plan to boil the Rice on the previous day and merely warm it the next morning, as then the washing can quick'y proceed. On no account allow the goods to lie damp, even for an hour, or the colors will run. Complete the whole operation at once. The brightest and most delicate goods of any material can be treated according to this method with the most pleasing success.

173.—FRENCH METHOD OF WASHING PIQUES AND PERCALES.

THE French method of washing piques and percales has always afforded very gratifying results. Prepare some rather warm, but not hot, lather of soft water and the best white soap. Wash the dresses through this lather, one at a time, but do not soak them. As soon as the first lather looks soiled, squeeze the dress from it, and at once wash it again through a fresh lather. When thoroughly clean, rinse in pure cold water, and lastly in water slightly blued. Squeeze, but not wring, the water completely from the dress, and hang it in a shady place to dry. The general hints (166) will give the proper way to iron piques and percales.

174.—TO BLEACH FADED ARTICLES.

MANY colored articles of the choicer kinds of material when too badly faded to be presentable, can be bleached and then worn or else used for other purposes.

Wash the articles well in very strong hot soapsuds, and then boil it until the color seems to be gone Again wash and rinse it, and dry it in the heat of the sun. If still not quite white, repeat the boiling. At this stage of the process, the goods may be subjected to the action of the Laundry "Bleach," (38), or treated according to the German Method of Bleaching White Goods, (40), and a clear and brilliant white will be the result.

175.—TREATMENT OF CHOICE TABLE-COVERS.

BRIGHT table-covers of cotton and worsted, silk and worsted, or printed cloth, can be done up easily and will look elegantly by this method. Prepare a soap liquid, by dissolving one bar of mottled soap and one pound of Pearlash in four gallons of scalding water. Have ready three tubs, and put in the first, one pailful of cold water and three gallons of soap liquid, in the second, one pailful of cold water and two gallons of soap liquid, and in the third, two pailfuls of cold water and one gallon of soap liquid. In another tub, prepare a rinsing water of six pailfuls of cold water with a tablespoonful of Oil of Vitriol in it. If it be a cotton and worsted cover, wash it through the three soap waters, rinse it through the Vitriol water for five minutes, and lastly rinse it out of clear cold water. Fold it smoothly, and without wringing, hang it up to drain dry.

For a silk and worsted cover, use the three soap waters and rub it well, but instead of the Vitriol water, rinse the cloth well in two pailfuls of water in which have been dissolved two pounds of common Salt. Rinse through two cold waters after the salted one, and hang the table-cover to dry in a warm room.

Wash a printed cloth through the three soap waters, rinse through two cold waters, with a tablespoonful of Oil of Vitriol in each, and then rinse through one clear cold water.

If a variety of table covers of different mixtures are to be washed, they may each be passed through the same soap waters, but use for each their own rinsing water. Always fold, drain, and dry quickly in a warm room, so the colors will not run into one another. To iron table covers, lay them under a damp sheet and press with a heavy sad-iron.

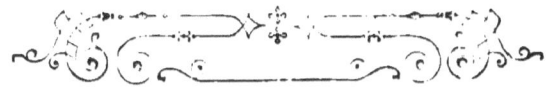

CHAPTER IX.

176.—WOOLENS AND FLANNELS.

IN doing up fine woolen articles, a little extra care will preserve their new, bright appearance and soft glossy finish. In a few details, articles of wool require a treatment in washing, different from goods of other material. The fibers are arranged differently, and are of a chemical composition, unlike the fibers of either cotton, linen, or silk. Examined under the microscope, wool fibers are found not to lay straight and regular, like those of cotton and linen, but on the contrary, are intricately interwoven and twisted around each other. Hence the peculiar laundry treatment these articles require. The process of rubbing, which may be applied to cotton and linen without injury, knots the fibers of the wool together and causes a thicking of the fabric, and consequently, a shrinking in its dimensions. In the case of woolens, therefore, rubbing should never be employed. Sluicing the article up and down in the water is the proper cleansing treatment.

Wringing also twists wool fibers out of place and causes fulling. The water should be pressed or squeezed out. Such is the chemical composition of wool, that soap coming in direct contact with the material, renders it harsh; and for this reason, woolens should always be washed in hot suds only, without Soda or washing crystals.

The temperature of the water in which flannels are immersed, is also a matter of importance. It should be neither cold nor scalding hot, and yet it should be as hot as the hand can bear. The several waters through which woolen articles pass—washing, rinsing, and blueing waters, should all be of the same temperature. If these peculiar demands of woolens and flannels are regarded when they are laundried, the results will be, they will not shrink, and the softness and original lustre will be preserved.

177.—TO REMOVE GREASE FROM WOOLENS AND FLANNELS.

PLACE underneath the article to be cleansed, a sheet of blotting paper or a woolen cloth; then rub the spot with some pure Benzoin, and the grease and dirt will disappear as if by magic. Be sure to place the blotting paper or the cloth, underneath the garment to be operated upon, otherwise, a circular stain will be left, very difficult of removal. The Benzoin drives the grease through the fabric, and it is absorbed by the paper placed underneath. After the spot is removed, still continue to rub till all the Benzoin evaporates. This must be done, or the Benzoin itself will leave a stain. Care should be taken in handling Benzoin (213).

178.—SPIRITS OF AMMONIA.

ANOTHER successful way of removing grease from woolen articles is, to rub the spot with a piece of flannel or a sponge moistened with Spirits of Ammonia. This method is especially adapted to cases where the grease has been long in the fabric. This alkali is the most effective agent known for removing grease from woolens. It unites with the grease to form a soap. which readily washes out with a little water.

179.—BLACK STAINS ON SCARLET WOOLEN GOODS.

PERSPIRATION generally leaves black stains upon red flannel, but the dark spots may be removed as follows: Mix Tartaric Acid with water, until the water acquires a pleasant taste. Then saturate the black spots with the acidulated water, taking care not to have it touch the clean part of the garment. Rinse the spot immediately in fair water. Weak Pearlash water is excellent to remove stains produced by acids. The Pearlash water should not be made so strong as to injure the fabric.

180.—SHRINKING FLANNELS.

PREVIOUS to making up flannel articles, it is well to shrink the material. The articles are then not so liable to shrink, nor will they require much attention in future washings. Soak the flannels first in cold hard water, and then in hot soft water. Then, without wringing, hang them up to drain dry. This process will shrink flannel so thoroughly, that it is not apt to full in subsequent washings.

181.—WHITE WOOLENS.

IF it be desired to keep white woolens from shrinking when washed, do not rub soap upon them, but make a good suds of hard soap, and wash the flannels in it. Wash them in a second suds; and then place them in a clean tub, and pour over sufficient warm water to cover them, and allow them to remain until the water becomes cold. A little Indigo in the warm water will give the woolens a brighter appearance. If it is desired to have the flannels shrink so as to make them thick, wash them in soft-soap suds, and then rinse them in cold water.

182.—COLORED WOOLENS.

WOOLENS of plain or variegated colors, have a strong tendency to fade in washing, and the colors are quite apt to mix. This difficulty may be guarded against, by immersing them in warm water containing a small quantity of Beef Gall, before permitting soap-suds to come in contact with them. A tablespoonful of Gall to a gallon of water, is about the right proportion to use (167).

183.—HOT SUDS FOR FLANNELS.

TO keep fine flannels soft and bright, they should be washed in clean hot suds. They will have a clearer and brighter appearance, if the suds be colored with a little bluing. They will be softer, if they are hung out directly from the suds, without being rinsed. Woolens of all kinds will be improved, if washed in rather hot suds.

184.—METHOD OF WASHING CHOICE WOOLENS AND FLANNELS.

PRIOR to washing, beat out of the articles any dust or mud adhering to them. Prepare some hot suds by cutting into slices good white soap, and boiling it in soft water. Do not use the suds boiling hot, but let it be as hot as the hand can bear, when the articles are put in. The woolens should not be rubbed with soap, nor should the material itself be rubbed. Sluice the article up and down in plenty of suds. In this manner, pass them through a suds several times, every time changing the suds, until they are perfectly clean; and then instead of wringing, squeeze out the suds water. Patent clothes wringers are a vast improvement upon hand labor, for this purpose, as without injury to the fabric, they press out the water so thoroughly, that the articles dry in considerable less time than after the most thorough hand wringing. After rinsing, squeeze out the water and dry in the open air, if the weather will admit of the articles drying quickly; otherwise, dry in a warm room, but avoid too close proximity to the fire.

185.—IRONING FLANNELS.

FINE flannel and woolen articles, which are desired to be particularly nice, may be made as soft, glossy and fuzzy as when they were new, provided the surface over which they are ironed is very soft, and provided a piece of damp cloth is laid over them, and this cloth pressed until it becomes dry. The iron should never come in direct contact with the woolen, as it will press down the nap so tightly, that the goods will have that old appearance that nearly always marks them when they have been once washed. This method of ironing is especially adapted to smoothing red flannels.

186.—WOOLEN BLANKETS.

INSTEAD of ironing large woolen blankets, it is an easier and better plan to treat them in the manner following: While they are just a trifle damp, fold them in large folds, and place them between two boards or table-leaves, and lay on the top a heavy weight. Let them remain in this position, until they are dry. This plan smoothes them better than the sad-iron.

187.—SCOTCH METHOD OF WASHING WOOLEN SHAWLS.

SCOTCH laundresses are noted for their skill in doing up fine plaid shawls, and the method they use is the following: Scrape finely, a pound of soap, and boil it down in sufficient water. As it cools, beat it with the hands till it becomes a sort of jelly. Then add three tablespoonfuls of Spirits of Turpentine, and one of Ammonia. Wash the shawl well in this mixture. Rinse in cold water, until all the soap is dissolved away, and then rinse in salt water. Fold it between two sheets, taking care not to allow two folds of the shawl to lie together. Use the salt in the rinsing water, in the case of bright colors only that are liable to run. In ironing them, place a piece of muslin between the shawl and the iron. Washed according to this method, plaid shawls will look as bright as new.

188.—TO CLEAN WOOLEN CLOTHES.

THIS is one of the best methods known for scouring woolen clothes. Mix half an ounce of Sulphuric Ether and half an ounce of Aqua Ammonia, with three ounces of soft water. Rub the article well with a sponge, frequently wetting the sponge in this mixture, until the dirt is removed. Then sponge with clean water. Next, lay over the article a coarse towel, which has been saturated with water and wrung out, and press the towel with a hot iron. While the steam is yet rising from the cloth, brush it down with a clothes brush; and the article will have a decidedly new appearance.

189.—TO WASH RED FLANNELS.

FLANNELS of the brightest red or scarlet, when soiled, can be washed by these directions, and they will never lose their color. Mix a handful of Flour and a quart of cold water together, and boil them for ten minutes. Add this to some warm suds, and wash the flannel gently, rinsing rather than rubbing it. Then rinse it through three or four warm waters. Soft, or Olive soap should be used for woolens, in preference to hard soap.

190.—TO PRODUCE A BEAUTIFUL WHITE ON FLANNELS.

FLANNEL turned yellow by age, may be whitened by soaking it for some time in a solution of hard soap, to which strong Ammonia has been added, and then drying in the sunshine. This is the process which manufactures employ for bleaching flannels, and the proportions they use are, one and a half pounds of hard soap, fifty pounds of salt water, and one and two-thirds pounds of strong Ammonia. For home use, the same proportions may be used, but reduced to suit the quantity of material to be bleached.

191.—A QUICK METHOD OF BLEACHING FLANNEL.

A BEAUTIFUL white may be reproduced on flannels turned yellow by age, in a shorter time than that required by the previous method.

Soak the flannel for a quarter of an hour in a dilute solution of Bisulphate of Soda, to which has been added, under constant stirring, a little dilute Hydrochloric acid. Keep a cover over the vessel containing the solution. After soaking the goods the allotted time, rinse them thoroughly in rather hot water. This last method is very speedy.

192.—TO RESTORE THE GLOSSY FINISH.

THE glossy finish of woolen goods is always removed by washing, but it may be restored by the accompanying plan. Brush over the cloth the way of the nap, with a brush dipped in very weak gum water, (28). Lay over it a sheet of paper or a piece of muslin, and place it under a weight or in a screw press until dry. This treatment is valuable for restoring the dull spot often left after washing out a stain. Of course, if the woolen articles are old and dingy, nothing could restore the original finish, but with new goods this method is successful.

193.—TO WHITEN FLANNEL OR WOOLEN HOSE.

WET the woolen yarn or hose with weak suds, wring it out, and then hang it on sticks or a cord stretched across a barrel, in the bottom of which powdered Brimstone or Sulphur is burning. Two tablespoonfuls of Brimstone is sufficient. The barrel must be tightly covered. If they are not white enough by one application, repeat the process. Hang the yarn in the open air for a day or so, to remove all odor of the Sulphur. Then wash the yarn and rinse it through blueing water. Be careful not to let the Sulphur blaze or scorch the hose.

194.—LAMBS' WOOL HOSE.

WORSTED or lamb's wool stockings or other knit articles should never be mended with unshrunken worsted or lamb's wool; because the latter being new it shrinks when washed more than the hose, and draws them up till the toes become short and narrow and the heel has no shape left. First wash the new yarn so that it will correspond with the old.

195.—"TUB-WASHING" AND BLEACHING WOOL.

IN bleaching wool it is essential to first free it from its natural grease. The following is the method used in large mills, where several tons are always cleansed in one scouring. This mill process is termed "tub-washing." It is needless to scour wool when it is intended to dye the yarn, but for nice white yarn, this process is very valuable. In using the alkaline lyes for this purpose, great caution should be exercised; for although wool is insoluble in water, it is capable of being dissolved by a strong alkali. Add to the scouring water enough Soda and Lye to render it alkaline; and boil it to about 120° Fahr., at which temperature add a little Aqua Ammonia. Next throw in the wool and stir it around with a stick. After stirring it awhile, pick up a small portion of the wool on the point of the stick and ascertain whether the wool be sufficiently clean. When well scoured, throw it upon a sieve and let it drain. Then place it where the sun will shine on it hotly, until it is perfectly dry. The rays of the sun will bleach it as white as snow. Sulphurous acid gas, or the fumes of burning Sulphur, are likewise employed for bleaching wool.

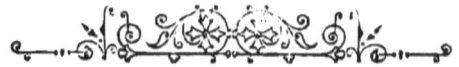

CHAPTER X.

196.—RENOVATION OF SILKS.

THE renovation of fine silks and silken articles is treated at length, because so few people understand how to handle this class of goods, or even believe that they can be successfully renovated. The costliest articles are regarded valueless, as soon as they become soiled. Placed in the skillful hands of the French *Couturiere*, however, how readily are they rendered bright and new. The methods employed are not difficult, they only require exact and careful execution. The wonderful changes which silk undergoes, from the time when the silk-worm spins its delicate cocoon, until the skill of man weaves it into costly and delicate articles, are indeed marvelous. It is no wonder that the renovation of silk is a nice operation.

197.—TO REMOVE GREASE SPOTS FROM SILKS.

TO accomplish this without injury to the color of the silk is some times easy, but more frequently very difficult. It is rarely ever impossible, however, if the proper means are employed. Much may depend upon skillful and persevering manipulations. A variety of the best agents known for this purpose is here presented. They cover nearly every possible case, and a lady can use her own judgment as to which is the most applicable to any particular case. The selection of the method to be used may depend somewhat upon the convenience with which its ingredients may be obtained. As far as possible, extract grease spots from silk while they are fresh, as they can then be more completely extracted than when they have become hardened in the fabric.

198.—FRENCH CHALK.

FRENCH Chalk is a fine soluble powder possessing a dry absorbing property, and acting upon silk like Fuller's Earth upon cloth.

To remove the grease spot from silk, grate a thick layer of French Chalk upon it. Common Chalk may be used, but it is not so good as French Chalk. Cover the layer of Chalk with brown paper, and apply a moderately hot iron, letting the iron remain until it becomes cold. Be careful not to have the iron so hot as to scorch or change the color of the silk. In this process, the heat of the iron melts the grease, and the Chalk absorbs it. On removing the iron, if the grease does not appear to be entirely out, grate on more Chalk and again apply the iron. Repeat the process, until the grease is completely extracted. If time is no object, apply the Chalk to the grease spot, and lay the silk away in a dark place. In a few days the spot will disappear. For delicate colors this plan is the best, as the hot iron might injure them. Grease may be extracted from paper, woolen goods, and floors also, by the French Chalk method.

199.—FRENCH SCOURING DROPS.

THIS preparation for removing grease from silk, is a favorite with the French laundress. It is made in two ways. First: Mix together Camphene, eight ounces; pure Alcohol, one ounce; Sulphuric Ether, one ounce; and Essence of Lemon, one drachm. Another way is to take Spirits of Wine, one pint; Ox Gall three ounces; and Essence of Lemon, a quarter of an ounce. If put away in bottles, tightly corked, these preparations will keep always ready for use. They are also excellent for removing grease from velvets.

200.—SIMPLE METHOD FOR REMOVING GREASE FROM SILKS.

THIS is a simple, convenient and valuable method. Separate a visiting or other card, and rub the grease spot with the soft internal part. The spot will disappear, without dulling the gloss of the silk. Be careful to rub the silk on the wrong side, as the card will sometimes soil silks of delicate colors. If this precaution be taken, the spot can not be seen on the right side of the silk.

201.—EGG METHOD.

SEPARATE as perfectly as possible the Yolk from the White of an Egg. Then spread out the silk on a table, and dip a soft clothes brush into the Yolk and rub the spot till the grease seems loosened. **The Yolk will not injure the most delicate colors, but the rubbing may, if too severe.** Then rinse in warm rain water: rub the edges with a damp cloth; and clap the whole between dry towels. If the stain has not quite disappeared, repeat the process. Grease may be extracted from broadcloth also, by this method, but it will not do so well for fabrics mixed with cotton and linen.

202.—DETERGENT FLUID.

THIS fluid is very good for removing grease spots from silks, velvets, and Satins. It is prepared by mixing together two ounces of rectified Spirits of Turpentine, and one fourth ounce each, of Absolute Alcohol and Sulphuric Ether. The fluid may be preserved for a long time in a bottle tightly corked. Shake it well before using, and apply with a sponge.

203.—AQUA AMMONIA.

AQUA AMMONIA is excellent to remove grease spots from silk, velvet, and in fact, any kind of fabric. Use the Ammonia nearly pure; then lay white blotting paper over the spot, and iron it gently. Salts of Ammonia mixed with Lime will restore silks stained with wine or vegetable juices. After the Ammonia effects the removal of the stains, it should be entirely removed with water.

204.—CHLOROFORM.

AS Chloroform will not injure the colors, it is very valuable for removing stains from silks or velvets. Dip a clean soft cotton rag in Chloroform, rub the spots rapidly but gently, and the grease will immediately disappear. If necessary, repeat the operation. Be careful to do the rubbing lightly and rapidly; and then finish with a clean dry cloth. If these precautions are not taken, a slight stain may be left by the Chloroform.

205.—ACID STAINS ON VIOLET SILK.

ANY acid dropped on violet silk destroys its color. The color may be restored by creating a new stain, and then removing both the old and new stain simultaneously. Wet the discolored part with Tincture of Iodine. After a few seconds, saturate the spot again with a solution of Hyposulphate of Soda, and dry gradually. The color will be perfectly restored.

206.—OX GALL.

OX GALL is a very delicate cleansing agent, and can be employed to remove grease spots from silk. It will also brighten the colors, (167.) Add one or two tablespoonfuls to a gallon of warm water. Immerse the article, or sponge the surface with the Ox Gall water, (168.)

207.—TO REMOVE WAX STAINS FROM SILK.

MIX powdered French Chalk with Lavender Water to the thickness of mustard. Apply it to the stain and rub it gently with the fingers or palm of the hand. Lay a sheet of clean blotting paper over the spot, and a sheet of brown paper over the blotting paper. Then run over the brown paper with a warm iron. When dry, remove the Chalk, and gently dust the silk with a white handkerchief. If a faint mark still remains, a second application of French Chalk and Lavender Water will remove it. If the wax has fallen thickly on the silk, first carefully remove all that is possible with a pen-knife.

208.—SPERMACETI, OLEIN, & STEARIN STAINS.

FIRST scrape off as much as possible with a penknife. Then lay a thin soft white blotting paper over the spots, and press it with a warm iron. By repeating this process, the stain may be entirely drawn out. Afterward rub the cloth where the spot has been with some soft brown paper.

209.—TO REMOVE RESIN SPOTS FROM SILKS.

STAINS produced by wax, resin, turpentine, pitch, or any substance of a resinous nature, may be removed by pure Alcohol. It often happens that when common Turpentine is employed to remove grease, varnish, or paint stains from silk, the Turpentine itself leaves a stain almost as objectionable as the original stain. These stains are due to the resin, which was held in solution by the Turpentine, and which remained in the silk after the volatile portion had evaporated. Alcohol applied with a clean sponge will remove such stains, because Alcohol will dissolve the resin. The stains should be first moistened with the Alcohol, and allowed to soak for a few minutes. Fresh Alcohol is again applied with a sponge, and with a light rubbing motion. Then wipe it as dry as possible, and hang it in the open air to finish drying.

210.—TO REMOVE PAINT FROM SILK OR VELVET.

THIS method is used to extract paint not only from silk and velvet, but also from goods of any material. Saturate the spots with rectified Spirits of Turpentine; and after it has remained several hours, rub the stained portion between the hands. The paint will crumble away, without any injury to the color or the texture of the fabric.

211.—OLD PITCH. VARNISH, OR OIL PAINT STAINS.

TO remove stains of this class after they have been long in the goods, it is necessary to moisten them with a little lard or butter, previous to applying Turpentine or soap. In such cases, a simple way is to soak the stains in Spirits of Turpentine, and when well moistened, to wash them with the same fluid. Benzoin is also excellent for this purpose; and Chloroform will remove paint from articles, when almost every other agent fails. Procure as pure Turpentine as possible, or it may itself leave a stain.

212.—BENZOIN STAINS.

IN removing grease spots from fabrics by the use of Benzoin or Turpentine, it often happens that a discolored or stained outline of the portion moistened remains. A layer of Gypsum, extending a little beyond the moistened region, will avoid this trouble. When the article dries, shake or brush off the Gypsum, and no trace of the stain will remain.

213.—CAUTION IN USING BENZOIN.

FROM the facility with which it removes grease from fabrics, this substance is regarded almost indispensable in the household. Few persons, however, realize the explosive character of Benzoin, or the dangers attending a careless use of it. It is very volatile and vaporizes with so great a rapidity, that the contents of a four ounce vial, if overturned, would render the air of a moderately sized room highly explosive. Too great care can not be taken in handling this substance in close proximity to a fire. It is well to remember, that the vapor escaping from an uncorked bottle, will cause a flame to leap over a space of several feet.

214.—WASHING SILKS.

TO wash silks successfully is a very nice operation. The finest and most delicate colored silk may be renovated, and made to look as good as new, provided proper care be taken and certain conditions are fulfilled. French dressmakers and laundresses are especially noted for their skill in managing silks; and any lady may equal them, provided the right treatment is understood.

215.—THE REQUISITE CONDITIONS TO BE FULFILLED.

ALL grease spots and stains should be extracted from silks before beginning to wash them; for when the whole of the garment is wet, the spots are apt to be invisible.

Use hard soap for all colors, except yellow, for which soft soap is best. Put the soap into hot water and beat it until dissolved, and then add sufficient cold water to make it just luke-warm. Put in the silk and rub it until clean; then take it out, without wringing, and rinse it in fair luke-warm water; then rinse again in another water.

Never wring or crush a piece of silk while it is wet: because the creases thus formed will remain forever, especially if the silk is thick and hard.

In rinsing, dip the silk up and down in the water; then take it out, without wringing, and hang in the shade to dry.

Fold them while damp and let them remain, so the moisture will penetrate evenly through all the parts. It is the best way to smooth them in a mangle; or if a mangle be not possessed, iron them on the wrong side with a sad-iron just warm enough to smooth them.

216.—PRESERVING THE COLORS.

IN washing silks, delicate colors are quite apt to mix or run. To effectually prevent this, different colors require different ingredients in the rinsing water.

For bright yellow, crimsons, and maroons, add to the rinsing water sufficient Sulphuric Acid to give the water an acid taste.

For the various shades of pink, use in the rinsing water a littler Vinegar, or Lemon Juice.

For scarlets, use a solution of Tin.

For purples, blues, and their various shades, use Pearlash. For olive greens, dissolve Verdigris in the rinsing water. Fawns and browns, should be rinsed in fair water. A little Alum dissolved in the last rinsing water, tends to prevent the colors of silks from mixing.

The water in which pared potatoes have been boiled is an excellent preparation in which to wash black silks. It stiffens and makes them glossy and black. Beef Gall and luke-warm water will also restore rusty black silks. They look better, not to be rinsed in clear water; but should be washed in two different waters.

217.—TO WASH SILKS.

FINE silks may be nicely cleansed by this method. Spread the article out smoothly upon a clean hard table or board. Soap well a piece of soft flannel, which has been previously wet with luke-warm water;

and rub with the flannel the surface of the silk one way, being careful that the rubbing is quite even. When the dirt is removed, rub off the soap with a sponge and plenty of cold water, of which the sponge must be made to imbibe as much as possible. As soon as one side is finished, treat the other in the same way. Not more of either surface should be done at a time, than can be spread perfectly flat upon the table, and the hand can conveniently reach. Likewise the soap should be sponged quite off one portion, before the soaped flannel is applied to another. The colors may be brightened by observing the directions given in method (216). White or colored satins and ribbons may also be cleansed by this method. It is a very effective process for renovating all kinds of silk ribbons and trimmings.

Red, purple, orange, blue, olive, and puce, are very much improved by this treatment, and it will not injure the delicate shades of lavender and green. If the silk to be washed is a dress, it is not necessary to rip the seams of the skirt; merely separate the band from the waist, and remove the lining at the bottom.

218.—POTATO LIQUOR.

COLORED or black silks, moreens, printed cottons, and chintzes, may be cleansed without injury to their colors by Potato Liquor. Grate raw potatoes to a fine pulp and mix them with water, in the proportion of one pint of water to one pound of Potatoes. Pass the liquid through a coarse sieve into a vessel, and let it remain until the fine white starch subsides to the bottom. Pour off the clear liquid, which is to be used for the cleansing. Spread the article to be washed upon a table, which should be covered with a linen cloth. Dip a sponge in the Potato Liquor, and apply it until the dirt is removed. Then rinse the article several times in clear cold water.

219.—BLACK REVIVER.

THE celebrated Black Reviver for restoring the color of black silk, cloth, or leather, is made as follows. Take of bruised Gall, four ounces; Logwood, Copperas, Iron Filings, free from grease, and Sumach Leaves, each one ounce. Put the Galls, Logwood, and Sumach Leaves, into one quart of good vinegar, and set the vessel containing the mixture into a warm water bath for twenty-four hours. Then add the Iron Filings, and Copperas, and for about a week occasionally shake the mixture. It should be preserved in a bottle well corked.

220.—HOW TO USE THE BLACK REVIVER.

IN using the Black Reviver on silks, first steep the silk for a few hours in cold water. Then put half a pint of the Reviver into half a gallon of water, and add a cupful of Ox Gall. Make the solution hot and sponge the silk. When it dries, smooth it with a warm iron. This preparation is excellent to restore rusty black silk. Rubbing the silk with Gin is also good.

The Black Reviver is much used to restore the black color of leather when it turns red.

Before the application, clean the leather well with soap and water. It is best applied with a sponge.

221.—HONEY MIXTURE.

THIS mixture is very useful for cleansing satins and colored woolen goods, as well as silks.

Mix well together, four ounces of soft soap; four ounces of Honey; the White of an Egg; and a wineglassful of Gin. Lay the article in widths on a hard surface, and thoroughly scour it with a rather stiff brush dipped in the Honey Mixture. Afterward rinse the article in cold water; let it drain partly dry, and iron it whilst quite damp, with a piece of thin muslin placed between the material and the iron, so that it may not be marked on the wrong side. In applying the mixture with a brush, lay the silk out smoothly on the table, so that every part may come under the brush.

White silk requires a little blueing in the water. Try this method. It is attended with perfect success.

222.—TO RENOVATE SILKS WITH OLD KID GLOVES.

THIS is a French method of renovating silks and its results are very pleasing. Especially in making over black silk dresses will it be found an excellent mode of cleansing them. Cut an old kid glove into small pieces, and pour over them a pint of boiling water. Cover the vessel containing the liquid, and let it stand where the water will keep warm, if possible. The next day, boil it again, strain it and add a dessert spoonful of Alcohol. Sponge the silk on the right side, keeping the liquid warm; and iron immediately on the wrong side, with an iron only moderately hot. By thus steeping the kid glove, certain portions are dissolved, and a decoction is obtained possessing admirable properties for restoring silks. For black silks, use a black kid glove; and for light shades of silk, use white or light kid gloves. For this purpose, it is well to save old kid gloves of various colors. The solution will answer without the Alcohol, but is much better with it. By this method, the silk is not only cleansed, but a beautiful lustre is added.

223.—SILKS SLIGHTLY SOILED.

WHEN silks are but slightly soiled, they may very frequently be renovated in the following simple way: Sponge the silk with warm water and soap; then place it on a hard board, and rub it dry with a dry cloth. Afterward iron it gently on the inside, using the hard board for an ironing surface.

Old black silk may be improved by sponging it with White Lye. In this case, the ironing must be done on the right side, a thin paper being placed under the iron to prevent glazing.

224.—SILK STOCKINGS.

WHITE, or silk stockings of fancy colors, will last twice the usual time, and can be kept soft and looking like new, if treated by the accompanying method.

Heat some soft water, and while it is on the fire cut into it slices of good yellow soap, sufficient to make a lather. Put in the stockings while the lather is warm. but not scalding hot, and wash them through two such lathers. A wineglassful of Gin in the first lather is an improvement, as it greatly facilitates in the removal of the dirt. Rinse them in luke-warm water, and then pass them through a water tinged with a little blueing.

Rose pink, (63), such as is used for fine muslins and laces, is better than the blueing. After rinsing, place the stockings between towels and let them get almost dry. Then lay them out on a small sheet very smooth and flat, just as they are when first purchased. Tack them to the sheet with a needle and thread, then turn the sheet over them, and pass them through the mangle. If it is not convenient to have them mangled, run between weighted rollers; the next best plan, is to put about six stockings, one upon the other, between muslin, lay them on a stone doorstep, and roll them in the same way that dough is rolled with a rolling pin. They should not be mangled or rolled in towels, as the pattern of the towels would be impressed upon them. If the stockings have lace fronts, they will more particularly require the tacking mentioned above to make them look nice. No Washing Soda or Crystal of any kind should be used. Do them as quickly as possible, and not leave them lying about. A good laundress takes as much pride in doing up a silk stocking elegantly, as she would a white vest.

225.—WASHING SILK SHAWLS.

MANY ladies never attempt to wash fine silk or woolen shaws. They are afraid to make the experiment, but by this simple method these articles may be washed without mixing the colors, and they will be as soft and bright as when first purchased. Pare and grate raw, mealy Potatoes, and add two quarts of cold water to every pint of the Potato pulp. Let it stand five hours, and then strain through a sieve, rubbing through as much of the Potato pulp as possible. Let the strained water settle again, and when very clear, carefully turn the water off from the dregs. Next place a clean white cotton sheet over a perfectly clean table, and lay on the shawl which is to be cleaned, and tightly pin it down. Dip a sponge that has never been used into the Potato water, and rub the shawl until it is clean. Then rinse in clean water, using in this rinsing water a teacupful of salt to every pailful of water. Next spread the shawl on a clean level place, where it will dry quickly. If hung up to dry, the colors are apt to run and the shawl will be rendered streaked. Fold it up while still damp and let it remain half an hour. Then either pass it through a mangle, or wrap it in a clean white sheet, and place it under a heavy weight till it becomes dry. If there are any grease spots on the shawl, it is best to remove them before the washing is begun.

226.—DAMASK AND BROCATELLO TAPESTRY.

TAPESTRY which has some parts raised above the ground, representing flowers and other figures, are usually considered difficult of renovation; but the richest and most elegant flowered curtain, either silk and cotton, silk and worsted, damask, terry, or brocatello, may be restored to nearly its original beauty by the accompanying treatment:

First dip the curtain into Camphene; then lay it on a board, and with a brush, rub it first on the wrong side and then on the right. Dip the curtain again into the Camphene, and then rinse it in some fresh Camphene. Let it drain a minute or two. Wipe it with a linen or cotton sheet till all the moisture possible is absorbed; and then brush it with a dry brush of soft hair. Hang it in the open air for a few hours to take away the odor of the Camphene. Dampen the curtain by placing it between moistened sheets. Iron with a damp cloth between the curtain and the iron. A gallon of Camphene is sufficient for each curtain width.

227.—SILK COVERINGS AND WORSTED REPS.

SILK or worsted rep furniture of any kind or color, may be freshened as follows: First place a sheet under each piece of furniture as it is cleaned, to catch the falling litter. Then dust Indian Meal over the article, and rub it with a stiff brush till it is clean. When silk cushions or silk coverings to furniture become dingy, rub dry bran on them gently with a woolen cloth, till they become clean.

CHAPTER XI.

228.—LACES, SATINS, AND VELVETS.

THIS may be appropriately styled the ornamental chapter, for it treats of the finest articles of a lady's wardrobe, laces, crapes, veils, satins, velvets, silk ribbons, trimmings, kid gloves and furs. It is obvious that the costlier the article, the more valuable will be a knowledge of the art of preserving and renovating it. Every spring, summer, autumn, and winter, goes forth from Worth, the Parisian *Artist de mode*, a change of fashions. "As well out of the world as out of fashion," so four times a year must a lady seek the aid of the dress-maker and milliner. In the bustle of changing and remodeling, how essential for economy is a perfect knowledge of the skillful renovation of costlier articles. In the matter of economy alone, the following methods recommend themselves. They are methods which the most skillful Parisian milliners, dressmakers and laundresses employ.

229.—TO CLEAR STARCH LACES.

STARCH for laces should be made thicker, and used hotter than for linens. After laces have been well washed and dried, dip them in the thick hot starch in such a way that every part may be thoroughly starched. Then press out the excess of starch, spread them out smoothly on a piece of linen, and roll the whole up together, allowing them to remain half an hour, when they will be dry enough to iron. Never clap laces between the hands, as it injures them. Cambrics do not require starch so thick as nets or laces. Cold or raw starch is preferable for book muslin, as some of this material has a thick clammy appearance if starched in boiled starch. Fine laces are frequently wound around a glass bottle to dry, as by this means they are kept from shrinking.

230.—IRONING LACES.

IT is far better not to iron laces at all, especially fine lace; but in the case of ordinary laces and worked muslin, it will sometimes answer to pass a cool iron over the back of the lace, with paper between the iron and the lace. Raised point can be laid face downward on several folds of flannel, and the ivory punch or lobster claw inserted behind the raised portions. This, however, is rather a delicate operation, and perhaps had better not be attempted, for in the old unwashed lace these portions are not so prominent.

To produce something of the same effect in ironing embroidery, ordinary lace, crochet, *guipure d' art*, antimacassars, &c., have several folds of flannel beneath, press the point of the sad-iron well into the raised portions, and iron on the wrong side.

231.—IRONING FINE LACES.

THE finer kind of laces require a special treatment for smoothing them. When the lace has been starched and dried and is ready to be smoothed, spread it out as evenly as possible on the ironing cloth, and pass over it, back and forth, as quickly as possible, a smooth round glass bottle containing hot water, giving the bottle such pressure as may be required to perfectly smooth the lace. Sometimes the lace may be passed over the bottle, care being taken to keep the lace even and smooth. Either way is much better than to smooth laces with a sad-iron, for the iron is apt to turn the lace yellow. In filling the bottle with hot water, do not fill too fast or the bottle may break.

232.—TO WASH WHITE SILK LACE, OR DELICATE BLOND.

MANY ladies may think this a rather long process, and one requiring too much care; but some blond lace is very delicate and valuable and cannot be roughly handled. By following the directions of this method, ladies will surely be pleased with the results.

Take a black bottle covered with clean linen or muslin, and wind the blond around it, not leaving the edge outward but cover it as you proceed, and secure the ends with a needle and thread. Set the bottle upright in a pan containing a strong lather made from white soap and very clear soft water. Place the pan in the sunshine, and gently with the hand rub the lather up and down on the lace. Keep it thus in the sunshine every day for a week, changing the lather daily, and always gently rubbing the lace every time the lather is renewed. At the end of the week, take the blond off the bottle, and without wringing, pin it backward and forward on a large pillow provided with a clean tight case. Every scallop must have a separate pin, or more than one, if the scallops are not very small. The plain edge must also be pinned down to make it straight and even. The pins should be of the smallest toilet size. When quite dry remove the blond from the pillow, but neither starch, iron, or press it, simply lay it in long loose folds and put it away in a paste-board box.

233.—REVIVING BLOND LACE.

QUITE frequently blond lace, although but little soiled, has a wilted appearance which makes it look almost ruined. In such cases, it is not necessary to go through the long operation required by the previous method. The lace when but slightly soiled, can generally be revived by breathing upon it, and then briskly shaking and flapping it. The process may be repeated several times.

234.—FINE THREAD LACE.

FINE thread lace may be washed in the same manner as the blond, (232), or the process may be modified a little. When the thread lace has been attached to the bottle, take some of the best Sweet Oil and thoroughly saturate the lace. Have ready in a kettle a strong lather of soft water and white Castile Soap. Fill the bottle with cold water to prevent its vaulting, then cork it well, and stand it upright in the suds. To prevent the bottle from shifting about and breaking while over the fire, tie a string around its neck and secure the string to the ears of the kettle Let it boil in the suds for an hour, or until the lace is clean and white all through. Then drain off the suds and dry the lace in the sunshine, keeping it still attached to the bottle. When dry, remove it from the bottle, and wind it around a white ribbon block; or lay it in long folds within a sheet of smooth white paper, and then press it in a large book for a few days. It is a good idea to add about twelve drops of Aqua Ammonia to the lather for washing laces.

235.—PARISIAN METHOD OF WASHING POINT LACE.

BY following the directions given in this method, ladies may wash and finish their own point lace as skillfully as the best French laundress. Prepare a basin of strong white Castile Soap suds, and add a teaspoonful of powdered Borax. Baste the lace to be washed very carefully upon two folds of flannel with fine cotton. Soak the lace thus arranged in the **soap** mixture for twenty hours, or longer if very dirty, changing the suds several times. Next lay it to rinse in clear soft water for about three hours, changing this water once. Do not wring it, but squeeze out the water, and place the flannel with the lace still attached to it, lace downward, upon two folds of dry flannel. Lay the flannel on a table and smooth it with a hot iron. During the entire operation the lace must remain basted to the flannel, and when it is pressed, must lie sandwiched between the dry and damp flannels, and pressed upon the latter. When the lace is perfectly dry, rip it off the flannel, and it will be found elegantly laundried.

236.—SUGAR SIZING FOR LACES.

A SOLUTION of white Sugar makes an admirable sizing for laces. Dissolve twelve lumps of pure white Sugar in a teacupful of hot water. More or less of this sizing can be prepared, according to the quantity of lace to be starched. Pour it into a pan and add a little blueing or Rose Pink, (63). Dip each piece of lace separately in the sizing; and instead of wringing, squeeze out the excess of sizing.

237.—CREAMY TINT.

THE choicest kinds of laces have a peculiar creamy tint. The more valuable the lace, the richer this creamy tint will be. This much prized tint can be easily imparted to almost any kind of white lace, and it will be a very clever imitation of the costly article. Simply sponge or dip the lace in cold coffee. The decoction should be made pure, from Mocha, or the genuine old Java. It must not be made too strong, however, or it will impart too brown a tint.

238.—MAGNESIA AND FRENCH CHALK.

FINE laces may sometimes be cleaned by covering them with French Chalk or Magnesia, and thus laying them away for a week. At the end of that time, brush off the powder, and often the lace comes out perfectly clean. This method is so simple and attended with so little trouble, that it is advisable to try it before resorting to more difficult expedients. In about two-thirds of the cases where it has been tried, it has proved highly successful.

239.—TO WASH BLACK LACE.

RUSTY black lace can be beautifully restored by this treatment. Dissolve Spirits of Wine and Borax, of each one teaspoonful, in half a teacupful of very soft water. Squeeze the lace through this liquid three or four times; then rinse it in a cup of hot water, in which a black kid glove has been steeped. After which, pull out the edges of the lace, and when it is nearly dry, press it in a heavy book for about two days.

240.—SILVER AND GOLD LACE.

THIS method will be found very valuable in cleaning regalia suits, or any silver and gold trimmings. Lay the lace out smoothly on a piece of woolen carpet or a woolen cloth, and brush it free from dust. Prepare the cleansing powder by burning Roche Alum, powdering it finely, and sifting it through a lawn sieve. Rub this powder over the lace with a fine brush. By thus doing the tarnish will be removed and the brightness restored, provided the threads of the lace are not too badly worn.

241.—TO WASH A WHITE LACE VEIL.

THERE is probably no article of fashion so easily soiled, and their successful renovation so little understood, as lace veils. They may be skillfully washed, however, without the slightest injury.

Prepare a good lather of white soap and clear soft water. Immerse the veil and let it gently simmer for a quarter of an hour; then take it out, but be sure not to rub or wring it, merely squeeze out the water. Rinse it through two cold waters with a few drops of liquid blue or Rose Pink, (63), in the last. Next starch the veil by passing it through some clear Gum-Arabic water, or some thin Rice water. Stretch it out evenly and pin it to dry on a clean linen cloth, making the edge as straight as possible, opening out all the scallops and fastening each with pins. When dry, lay a piece of thin muslin over it, and iron on the wrong side.

242.—TO WASH A BLACK LACE VEIL.

TO a quantity of Ox Gall, add hot water sufficient to render it as hot as the hand can bear, and it is well to add a little Musk to perfume the Ox Gall. Pass the veil through this water, squeezing but not rubbing it; and rinse through two cold waters, tinging the last with a little Blueing. After it is dry, dress it in a sizing prepared by pouring boiling water on a small piece of Glue, (30); then squeeze it through this sizing, and pin it out to dry on a linen cloth, laying it very straight and even, and taking care to evenly pin the edges. When it dries, iron it on the wrong side, having laid a linen cloth over the ironing blanket. Any article of black lace may be washed by the same process.

243.—TO REMOVE STAINS FROM BLACK CRAPE.

BY this method stains can be removed not only from black crape, but from mourning dresses also. Boil a handful of Fig Leaves in two quarts of water until the decoction evaporates to a pint, then press out the leaves, strain the liquid, and bottle for use. Crape, mourning dresses, bombazines, &c., need only to be rubbed with a sponge dipped in this liquid, and the desired effect will be instantly produced.

244.—TO RESTORE RUSTY ITALIAN CRAPE.

HEAT half a pint of Skim Milk and water in equal proportions, and when scalding hot, dissolve in it a piece of Glue an inch square, and then remove from the fire. First clean the crape by rinsing it in Vinegar, and then stiffen it by dipping it in Milk solution. Squeeze it out and clap it till dry, and then smooth it with a hot iron. A sheet of paper should always be laid over it when it is ironed.

Gin is also excellent to restore rusty black crape. Dip it in and let it become saturated with the Gin. Then clap it dry, and smooth it out with a moderately hot iron. Italian crape may also be died to look as bright as new.

245.—WATER STAINS ON BLACK CRAPE.

WHEN a drop of water falls on a black crape veil or collar, it leaves a conspicuous white mark. These marks may be obliterated as follows: Spread the crape out on a table and place a large book on it to keep it steady, and lay a piece of old black silk underneath the stain. With a large camel's hair brush dipped in common black ink, go over the stain, and then wipe off the ink with a bit of old soft silk. It will dry immediately and the white stain will be no longer visible.

246.—TO WASH A CHINA CRAPE SCARF.

WHEN the fabric is good, these articles of dress can be washed as frequently as may be required, and no diminution of their beauty will be discoverable, even when among other colors of the pattern, the delicate shades of green are employed.

Make a strong lather of white soap and boiling soft water, and allow it to cool. When cold, or nearly so, wash the scarf quickly and thoroughly in it; then dip it immediately in cold hard water, in which a little Salt has been dissolved to preserve the colors. Give it another rinsing, and squeeze out the water, and hang it out to dry in the open air. Always pin it at its extreme edges to the line, so that it may not be folded together in any of its parts. The more rapidly the scarf dries the clearer and brighter will it appear.

247.—RIBBONS, VELVETS AND SATINS.

VELVETS, satins, silk ribbons, and trimmings, require nearly the same treatment as is applied to silks for removing grease, spots. The methods for washing this class of goods are also similar to the silk methods. To avoid needless repetition, ladies are referred to the various silk methods, (197) to (221), whenever they may have occasion to renovate velvets, satins, or ribbons. A few methods, however, are especially adapted to these materials.

248.—SOILED RIBBON.

A MIXTURE of Alcohol and finely rectified Benzoin is excellent for cleaning soiled ribbons. It is applied with a clean sponge. Be careful not to get near a fire or burning lamp, under penalty of an explosion, (213). Colors taken out by acids or vegetable juices may be readily restored by the use of Aqua Ammonia; which may be applied to any fabric or color without doing the least injury.

249.—ISINGLASS SIZING.

ISINGLASS sizing is much used to impart to ribbons gauze, or silk scarfs, a fine gloss and finish. After the dirt, grease spots and stains have been removed, rinse the article thoroughly in water, in which has been mingled a little Isinglass Starch, prepared as in method (31). Gum Arabic Starch, (28), is also good for the same purpose.

250.—CREASED RIBBONS.

TO restore creased ribbons, lay them out smoothly on a clean board, and dampen them evenly all over with water, using a very clean sponge. Roll them smoothly and tightly on a ribbon block of greater width than the ribbon and let them remain until dry. Wrap them in brown paper, and lay them away until wanted.

251—WRINKLES IN SILK SCARFS AND HANDKERCHIEFS.

THIS is a very good way to remove wrinkles from silk scarfs and handkerchiefs. Moisten the surface evenly with a sponge and some Wheat Glue, and then fasten the article with toilet pins, around the shelves or on a mattress, taking pains to draw out the article as smoothly as possible. When dry, the wrinkles will be invisible. Some silk articles are much improved when moistened with Glue or Gum Water, which must be very weak.

252.—TO STIFFEN SILK TRIMMINGS.

SPONGE the surface of the silk with a very weak Gum Arabic solution, (28); or with equal parts of Ale and water, and iron on the wrong side while it is damp. These are favorite methods with milliners, and are largely employed when old silks are used for trimmings, and it is desired that they should be particularly stiff.

253.—WRAPPING RIBBONS.

WHEN laying ribbons away in drawers, it is a bad plan to wrap them in newspapers. The Chloride of Lime used in the manufacture of white paper and newspapers is quite apt to bleach or fade delicate colors. Use instead, some soft brown paper. White or light shades of ribbon and satin, when laid away, should be wrapped first in blue tissue paper, and then with brown paper on the outside. For wrapping any delicate colored goods, the smooth yellow Indian paper is the best that can be used.

254.—TO EXTRACT GREASE FROM VELVET AND SATIN.

POUR a little Turpentine over the spot and rub it briskly with a piece of clean dry flannel, until the spot becomes quite dry. If the first application is not successful, repeat the operation; then brush the place well and hang the article in the open air, so that the unpleasant odor of the Turpentine may be removed.

255.—TO RAISE THE PILE ON VELVET.

THE pile or plush of velvet when pressed down may be easily raised and made to appear as glossy as when new. Hold the wrong side of the velvet over the steam arising from the boiling water until the pile rises. Another way is to lightly dampen the wrong side of the velvet, and hold it over a pretty hot iron but yet not hot enough to scorch. The steam arising will penetrate the velvet and the plush may be raised with a brush. Still another way, is to place a clean hot brick upon a wet cloth; hold over the velvet, and the steam will raise the pile. To give the gloss, rub well between the hands a small quantity of pure Lard, which must be entirely free from salt. Use only enough Lard to barely oil the hands. Lay the velvet out smoothly on a table, and gently pass the oily hands over the plush side. This will restore the glossy appearance, and can be used for either silk velvet, or velveteen.

256.—TO CLEAN WHITE & FLOWERED SATINS.

PREPARE a mixture of equal parts of sifted stale Bread Crumbs and powdered Blue. Thoroughly rub the satin all over with this mixture; then shake it well and dust it off with a clean soft cloth. If the satin is embellished with gold or silver flowers, rub the flowered portion with a piece of soft ingrain velvet, which will restore it to its original lustre. Next pass the satin through a solution of fine white hard soap, at a hand heat, drawing the satin through the hand.

Rinse in lukewarm water, dry it, and finish by pinning it out smoothly. Brush the flossy or bright side with a clean clothes brush, the way of the nap. Impart a finish by dipping a sponge into sizing, prepared by boiling Isinglass in water, (31), and rubbing the wrong side. Rinse a second time, use the brush again, and dry near the fire or in a warm room. Silks also may be cleansed by this method, but dispense with the brushing process.

257.—KID GLOVES.

FEW ladies are aware that kid gloves can be renovated as perfectly as any other article, yet such is a fact. The methods presented in this department are easy to follow, and will afford admirable results. It will be found the most economical to purchase the very best quality of kid gloves, for whenever they become soiled they can be readily cleansed and be made as good as new. Good gloves can be renovated a number of times, until they are worn out. They will thus outlast several pair of cheap gloves. Ladies who wear kid gloves in hot weather and who perspire freely, will find that injury to the gloves may be prevented if they will apply to the hands before drawing on the gloves, common dry Corn Starch.

258.—STAINS ON KID GLOVES.

STAINS may be removed even from the most delicate colored gloves, by suspending them for a day in an atmosphere of Ammonia. This may be accomplished by placing strong Aqua Ammonia in the bottom of a tall glass cylinder or a glass fruit can. Be careful to remove from the sides of the jar, any of the Ammonia which may spatter upon them. Attach the gloves to the stopper and suspend them in the jar, and the Ammonia gas will neutralize the stains. The gloves, however, must not come in contact with the liquid Ammonia.

259.—WASHING KID GLOVES.

WHEN kid gloves are so badly soiled that they require washing, the following method will be found very valuable. Old kid gloves will look nearly new, they will be soft, glossy, smooth, elastic and possess a good shape. Spread out the glove smoothly and neatly on a cloth folded three or four times. Have ready a little new Milk in one saucer and a piece of nice hard Soap in another. Dip a piece of soft flannel in the Milk, and with the flannel thus moistened, rub off a goodly quantity of the Soap, and begin to rub the glove downward towards the fingers, holding it firmly with the left hand. Continue this process until the glove, if white, looks of a dingy color, although clean; or if colored, until dark and spoiled. Lay them away to dry, or what is better, place them on the hand and rub them dry with a piece of soft flannel. They will soon look like new gloves.

260.—FRENCH KID GLOVES.

THIS method of cleaning French kid gloves is the one practiced in Paris, and for a long time the secret was zealously guarded. Since its introduction in this country, thousands of dollars have been saved. The method is exceedingly simple. Draw the gloves on the hands and wash them in some Spirits of Turpentine until they become quite clean. Wash them just as if you were washing your hands. When clean, hang them in a warm place to dry, or better, where there is a current of air, and the unpleasant Turpentine odor will disappear.

261.—TO CLEANSE GLOVES WITHOUT WETTING.

IT may be an advantage to cleanse gloves without wetting them, as it would be impossible for them to shrink. Make a mixture of dried Fuller's Earth and powdered Alum in equal parts, and having laid the gloves upon a clean board, apply the mixture on each side with a common stiff brush; then dust off the powder, and sprinkle them well with dry Bran and Whiting, and again dust them. This treatment, if they are not exceedingly greasy, will render them quite clean. If they are much soiled take out the grease with Crumbs of toasted Bread and powder of burnt Bone; then pass them over with a woolen cloth dipped in Fuller's Earth, or Alum powder. In this manner they may be cleansed without wetting them.

262—OPERA GLOVES, OR KID GLOVES OF LIGHT SHADES

LADIES are well aware how readily opera kid gloves become soiled. They can rarely be worn but once, for nearly every thing with which they come in contact leaves its mark. Those who are fond of wearing kid gloves of this style, can appreciate a successful method of renovating them.

Magnesia, Moist Bread and India Rubber are each good to clean kid gloves of light color. The substance should be thoroughly rubbed on the glove, and when brushed off, the glove will be found quite clean. Sometimes, however, gloves of very delicate shades are so badly soiled that they cannot be cleaned by this treatment. In such cases the color may be changed by dyeing them with a decoction of Saffron. The color will then be changed to yellow or brown, according to the strength of the Saffron decoction. Prepare the decoction by steeping Saffron in boiling water for about twelve hours. The top edges of the gloves must be well sewed together, to prevent the dye from staining the insides, and the best way of applying the dye is with a sponge. A teacupful of the Saffron decoction will be found sufficient for one pair of gloves.

263.—GENLEINE.

GANLEINE is a French composition for cleaning kid gloves. Dissolve three Troy ounces of Soap by heat in two ounces of water, and when nearly cold add two ounces of Javelle Water, (57), and one drachm of Aqua Ammonia. Work the whole into a paste, which is to be rubbed over the glove with flannel until it is sufficiently clean.

264.—EXCELLENT PERFUME FOR GLOVES.

TAKE of Damask or Rose Scent, half an ounce; Spirit of Cloves and Mace, each a drachm; Frankincense, a quarter of an ounce. Mix them well together and lay them in papers, and when hard press the gloves between them. The gloves will take the perfume in twenty-four hours, and hardly ever loose it. (132).

265.—FURS.

IN cleaning furs, strip them of their stuffing and binding, and lay them in as flat a position as possible. They should then be subjected to a very brisk brushing with a stiff clothes brush. After the brushing, any moth-eaten parts must be cut out, and neatly replaced with bits of new fur to match.

266.—SABLE, CHINCHILLA, SQUIRREL, FITCH.

FURS of these varieties should be treated as follows: Warm a quantity of new Bran in a pan and actively stir it to keep it from burning. When well warmed rub it strongly into the fur with the hand. Repeat the rubbing two or three times; then shake the fur well and give it a sharp brushing to entirely free it from dust.

267.—WHITE FURS, ERMINE, MINEVER, ETC.

LAY the fur on the table and rub it well with Bran moistened with warm water. Rub the fur with the moist Bran until the Bran becomes dry, and then rub it again with the dry Bran. The wet Bran should be put on with flannel, and the dry with a piece of book muslin. Light furs, in addition to the above, should be well rubbed with Magnesia, or a piece of book muslin, after the Bran process. Dry Flour may be used in place of the wet Bran. It requires a very thorough rubbing to clean ermine and minever, and they should always be rubbed against the way of the fur.

268.—STRETCHING.

FURS are usually much improved by stretching, which may be managed as follows. Dissolve three ounces of Salt in a pint of soft water. Strip the fur of its binding and stuffing, and then with this solution sponge the inside of the skin until it becomes thoroughly saturated. Care must be taken, however, not to wet the fur itself. Next lay it carefully on a board, with the fur side downward in its natural position. Now stretch it as much as it will bear to the required shape, and fasten with small tacks. The drying may be hastened by placing the skin at a little distance from the fire, where the warmth will strike it.

269.—TO PREVENT MOTHS IN FURS.

IN the month of April or May, beat fur garments well with a small cane or elastic stick. Lap them up in linen, without pressing the fur too hard, and put small lumps of Camphor between the folds. Lay the fur away in this state, in well closed boxes. When the furs are wanted for use again, beat them well and expose them to the air for twenty-four hours, and the unpleasant odor of the Camphor will disappear. If the fur has long hair, as beaver or fox, mix with the Camphor an equal quantity of strong Black Pepper in powder. A keg in which whiskey has been kept, is the most reliable place to put away furs during the summer.

CHAPTER XII.

270.—GENTLEMEN'S CLOTHING.

LADIES are naturally very apt in renovating their wearing apparel, but many ladies, compelled perhaps by necessity, or induced by a prudential turn of mind, closely study such economy, and from continual practice a wonderful skill and adroitness is attained. They seldom purchase new clothes, yet these ladies dress in excellent taste, and their wardrobe is as complete as one upon which three times more money has been expended. To but few persons, however, does it ever occur that gentlemen's clothing can be just as advantageously renovated. Whenever their clothes become a little rusty, gentlemen usually purchase a new suit, never thinking that by proper renovation a second service could be obtained from the old one. By skillful management, garments which have become too shabby even for wearing about home or while at work can be readily converted into respectable sunday clothes; even where they have worn glossy or threadbare, the original appearance can be restored. A small unpretending sign, "Gentlemen's Clothes Cleaned and Repaired," may be seen in every city of the civilized world. In these little clothes-cleansing establishments, constant experience determines the very best methods to employ. A careful treatment according to the methods here presented, will produce a wonderful change in the appearance of old clothes.

271.—GREASE SPOTS.

GREASE is the most common cause of gentlemen's clothes becoming soiled, and the spots usually disfigure the clothes more than anything else, for the grease not only spreads over a large surface, but the dust which invariably settles on it becomes incorporated with the grease, and adds to the disfigurement. Various agents are used for removing grease spots, but the disadvantage with most of them is, they do not entirely extract the grease. The spots may be invisible for a time, yet they soon reappear. Benzoin is extensively used and with good success. A very genteel old gentleman, whose clothes always appeared new and seemed to never wear out, when asked how he kept them looking so well, answered, that he bought Benzoin instead of new clothes. He had not bought a new suit for four years, but every year he bought a gallon of Benzoin.

272.—PEARLASH AND LIME LIQUID.

THIS liquid thoroughly extracts all the grease from the cloth, and the method is one of the best known for this purpose. To certain vegetable colors, however, it is highly destructive, and in such cases should never be used; for other colors it is entirely harmless. Dissolve one quart of Lime in as much soft water as will dissolve the Lime and leave about a quart of clear water, after the solution has been well stirred and allowed to settle. Let it stand about two hours, and then decant the clear liquid from the dregs into another vessel. Now add to this clear liquid half an ounce of Pearlash; stir the mixture, and when it settles bottle for use. Before using, the liquid should be diluted with water to adapt it to the strength or delicacy of the color of the cloth. It is applied with a coarse sponge, rubbing out the grease, and rinsing with clear water afterward.

273.—TO REMOVE ACID STAINS.

NOTHING can be better than Chloroform to restore the color of garments when destroyed by acids.

When any acid has accidently or otherwise destroyed or changed the color of a garment, Aqua Ammonia should first be applied to neutralize the stain. A subsequent application of Chloroform will then restore the original color (204). As far as possible, treat the stain as soon as the accident happens.

274.—TO REMOVE ALKALINE STAINS.

SODA, lye, and many other alkalies produce stains upon dark garments. Such stains can generally be made to disappear by the prompt application of Acetic Acid. When the cause of any stain is known to be an alkali, saturate the spot with Acetic Acid, and the Acid should then be entirely removed by a liberal application of water. Pure Cider Vinegar may be used instead of Acetic Acid.

275.—TO REMOVE PAINT AND WAX STAINS.

FIRST remove with a knife, as much of the wax as possible, without injury to the cloth. Drop a little Benzoin on the stain and rub it gently with a sponge repeating this process until the stain disappears. Stains caused by substances of a resinous nature, as turpentine, pitch, resin, &c., may be removed by pure Alcohol. To remove paint or varnish, Chloroform is the most successful agent that can be employed, (211) (204).

276.—STAIN METHOD FOR GENERAL APPLICATION.

THIS method will remove stains of various kinds from broadcloth, and in a great many cases will prove quite sufficient. Take an ounce of Pipe Clay that has been ground very fine, and mix it with twelve drops of pure Alcohol and the same quantity of Rectified Spirits of Turpentine. When it is desired to remove a stain from broadcloth, moisten a little of this mixture with Alcohol, and rub it on the spot; let it remain until dry, and when the powder is brushed off it will be found that the stain has disappeared.

The removal of stains is very thoroughly considered in the chapter on silks. Many of the methods there presented would apply equally as well to gentlemen's clothing. It is unnecessary to repeat them here, but in case of stains in gentlemen's, clothes which do seem to be covered by the methods in this department, the stain methods for silks (197) to (211), may profitably be consulted.

277.—METHOD OF CLEANSING BROADCLOTH.

THIS method for cleaning, or rather washing gentlemen's garments, is presented with the assurance that it will give the very best of satisfaction, as it is one of the most effective methods that can be employed. Dissolve half a pound of Saleratus and one Beef Gall in four gallons of warm water. Lay the garment on a table and scour it thoroughly in every part with a clothes brush dipped in this mixture; the collar of a coat and the grease spots must be repeatedly rubbed, the brush being frequently dipped in the mixture. When this has been done, rinse the article up and down in the mixture; then rinse it up and down in a tub of cold soft water, and without wringing or pressing, hang it where there is a current of air to drain and dry. Fasten a coat up by the collar, and as it dries shake it occasionally and pull it into its proper shape to prevent it from shrinking. When perfectly dry, it is sometimes the case with coats that nothing more is needed; in other cases it may be necessary to dampen the parts which look wrinkled, and either pull them out smooth with the fingers or press them with a warm iron, placing a piece of bombazine or thick woolen cloth between the iron and the article. Finish by thoroughly airing. For dark colored cloth garments, it is a good plan to add some Fuller's Earth to the Gall mixture. When nearly dry, the nap should be laid the right way and the garment carefully pressed; after which, a brush moistened with a drop or two of Olive Oil, should be passed over it several times, which will give it a fine finish. Garments cleansed in this manner, provided the directions be strictly followed, will look just as well as new. We have often seen it tried with unfailing success.

278.—COLORED PANTALOONS.

COLORED pantaloons look very well when washed as follows: Add one Beef Gall to about four gallons of fair warm water, and wash the pantloons in this mixture without using soap. Without wringing, hang them up to drain until partly dry, then lay them on a hard surface, and press them on the wrong side while slightly damp.

279.—CLEANSING GARMENTS WITH SOAP BARK.

IN tropical countries there are trees bearing red saponaceous berries, which the inhabitants use as a substitute for soap in washing clothes; the bruised bark also produces a lather like soap, on being agitated in water. The detergent properties of Soap Bark are superior to soap, and it can be freely used on fine fabrics and delicate colors which would be injured by soap. So great is its value for cleansing purposes, that the ground bark is now an article of commerce and can be found in any drug store. It is admirable for cleaning cashmeres of delicate shades, silks and woolen goods; the greasiest coat collar, when other agents fail, can be perfectly cleansed by its use, and it will render the sorriest old felt hat soiled with dirt and grease, as good as new. Soap Bark is prepared and used as follows: Dissolve a tablespoonful in a teacupful of boiling soft water. Any quantity in similar proportions, may be prepared and bottled for future use, and it is a good plan to always keep a bottle of it in the house. It is applied with a sponge, rubbing the article until it is saturated, and then rinsing in clear water. The solution is more effective when applied as hot as the hand can bear. It can be freely used on any white goods, and is entirely harmless to the finest colors. Five cents worth of Soap Bark will renovate a gentleman's whole wardrobe.

280.—TO RENOVATE RUSTY BLACK CLOTH.

DISSOLVE an ounce of Aniline Black in a bowlful of boiling water. First sponge the articles well with soap and hot water, rubbing the nap down with the sponge; then sponge them all over with the Aniline Dye, being careful to keep them smooth and to brush downward. In this simple manner, faded or rusty black clothes can be given a perfect black, and the color will not crock or rub off.

281.—TO RAISE THE NAP ON CLOTH.

WHEN cloth has worn glossy its original appearance can be restored by this method, or even where it has worn threadbare the nap may be raised. Soak the garment about an hour in cold water, which will swell the fibres and cause it to thicken. Now put it on a hard surface and rub the threadbare portion with a half-worn hatter's card, or a prickly thistle until the nap is raised. Hang it up to dry and with a stiff brush lay the nap the right way.

282.—SPRINGING PANTS.

IT is well known that pants made by a regular tailor have a much superior set than when made by a tailoress. The chief point of superiority is the perfect spring at the ankles, by which the pants curve out symmetrically and hang faultlessly over the shoes. There is no reason, however, why a lady should not be able to accomplish this; it requires a little strength and that is about all. It may be done as follows, with an ordinary sad-iron. The front half on each leg only is sprung and the spring begins about seven or eight inches from the bottom. Fold the cloth in the length exposing the wrong side, and as the outside seam is farther in front than the inside seam have the fold a third nearer the outside edge, so that the spring may be directly in front. Make the cloth quite damp and have the iron as hot as possible without scorching. Pressing the iron upon the cloth with the right hand, pull the cloth with the left using considerable strength, and at the same time give the iron a twisting movement, until the required curve is sprung. By making an experiment upon a piece of cloth it will be seen how readily cloth may be sprung.

The Corrugated Glossing Iron (13,) is well adapted for springing cloth, for in the twisting process, the ridges hold the cloth without slipping. Cut after a good pattern and properly sprung, pants made at home will set as elegantly as when made by the fashionable merchant tailor.

283.—PRESSING PANTS.

NEW pants, no matter how good the material or how well made, soon draw up and become baggy at the knees. This difficulty may be easily remedied. Draw each leg over a narrow press board, dampen the goods, and press out the sag with a hot iron, having an old cotton cloth between the material and the iron, to prevent scorching or glazing. After the pants have once drawn up and been pressed out, the sags are not so liable to return.

284.—MAKING OLD CLOTHES NEW.

TURNING garments is an ingenious way of making them last a long time. Shabby coats, overcoats, vests, pants, and even old faded hats, when the cloth is reversible, may be readily turned and the result is a new article. There are large firms engaged in this business; cast-off clothing is bought up and after being skillfully turned is sold again as new goods, the most acute observer failing to detect the fraud. Now if you are liable to buy an old garment that has thus been made new, would it not be advisable to have the turning done at home and receive the benefit of the economy. The process is very simple and the expense trifling. Take off the binding and separate the outside cloth from the lining, then rip the seams apart and reverse the cloth, thus exposing the bright new side. No cutting or fitting is required, and it is only necessary to attach the cloth to the same lining again, sew on new binding and buttons, and the result is a bran new garment. The only care to be taken is in reversing the buttonholes, but this may be done so neatly that they will never show that they have been worked over; or the buttonholes may be sewed together and the buttons sewed above them and then new buttonholes worked in the other side. Very frequently the wrong side has a different color, and when turned an intimate friend would admire the new suit. Twilled and basket goods and also blue flannel or other woolen goods that have a finish on the wrong side may be profitably reversed; and in a similar manner a soft felt hat may be turned. This process is better than cleaning or dyeing. Ladies are ever turning their wearing apparel, why not treat gentlemen's clothes with the same prudent regard. Try it and the result will be astonishing. The great economy to be gained surely recommends this prooess.

CHAPTER XIII.

285.—RENOVATION OF CARPETS.

TO most gentlemen house cleaning is associated with cold dinners and a grand uproar. No doubt the ordeal is as great for ladies; and the methods in this department are presented with the confidence that they will be welcome. It is on such occasions that the city husband appreciates the amenities of city life, for in nearly every large city there are men whose sole occupation is the renovation of carpets. They are professional carpet cleaners and do a thriving business. Under their skillful management the most soiled ingrain, tapestry, Brussels, or Turkish carpet is renovated, and no one would know but what it was a new carpet. They go to a dwelling, take up the carpet, thoroughly renovate it and place it on the floor again, looking like a carpet fresh from the store; the entire work being done in an incredibly short time. The secret of their success in making soiled carpets look so well is, that although the carpets are thoroughly washed and rinsed they are at no stage of the operation allowed to become soaked through. The following is the process, a little modified to adapt it for home use.

286.—CARPET CLEANERS' METHOD.

WHEN the carpet is taken up, hang it on a line or lay it on the grass and whip it first on one side and then on the other, with pliant whips until entirely free from dust. Have the floor thoroughly scoured and dried and tack down the carpet firmly. If the carpet is so much soiled as to require further cleaning proceed as follows. Take a pailful of cold spring water and put into it about three gills of Ox Gall; and take a second pailful of clear cold water and add sufficient Vinegar to produce a sour taste. Now with a soft scrubbing brush, rub some of the Ox Gall Water upon the carpet and scour briskly, which will raise a lather; then wash the lather off with a sponge dipped in the Vinegar Water. To prevent the carpet from being soaked through, scour only a yard square at a time. Frequently change the Vinegar Water. As soon as the lather is removed rub the carpet with a clean dry cloth. When the washing is finished, open the windows to allow the carpet to dry more quickly. Any particularly dirty spots should be rubbed with nearly pure Gall. A carpet treated in this manner will be greatly refreshed in colors, particularly the greens.

287.—GREASE SPOTS.

THE method employed by carpet cleaners for extracting grease spots is very speedy and simple. Grate on the spots a thick layer of Potter's Clay, cover it with a sheet of brown paper and set on a warm iron. The heat of the iron melts the grease and the Potter's Clay absorbs it, and the powder can be afterwards swept off. It may be necessary to repeat the process several times to extract all the grease. Care should be taken not to have the iron too hot, try it first on a piece of white paper, if it turn the paper brown or scorch it in the least, it is too hot.

288.—BORAX WATER.

ANOTHER effectual way to extract grease spots from carpets is by the use of Borax Water. Mix a little soap in a gallon of soft water and add an ounce of Borax. Wash the spots well with this solution, applying it with a piece of clean soft flannel, and the grease spots will soon disappear. If there are grease spots on the floor, remove them with Potter's Clay, (299), before the carpet is tacked down.

289.—OIL ON CARPETS.

WHENEVER oil is spilt on carpets apply as soon as possible plenty of Wheat Flour or Whiting, which will absorb the oil and keep it from spreading. If the oil is near the seams rip them apart and put Whiting on the floor under the carpet. Next day sweep up all the Flour above and under the carpet, and if the oil has not entirely disappeared, again apply the Flour.

290.—MAGNESIA PASTE.

ALMOST any kind of grease spots may be removed from carpets by Magnesia Paste. Scrape and pound together Magnesia in the lump and Fuller's Earth, equal quantities of each, and after the ingredients are well mixed, pour over them a quantity of boiling water, sufficient to convert them into a paste. Lay the paste as hot as possible upon the grease spots and after it has remained about a day, and the composition has become dry, brush it off and it will be found that the spots have disappeared, (238). This method is valuable, especially for Brussels or carpets of thick texture.

291.—CARPETS SLIGHTLY SOILED.

OFTEN Carpets that are but slightly soiled may be cleaned and brightened by this simple treatment. After the dust has been thoroughly whipped out, spread the carpet on the clean dry floor and tack it down. Pare some raw potatoes and grate them over the carpet, then rub them about with a new broom, which process will refresh the carpet greatly. Let it become thoroughly dry before walking on it.

292.—TO PREVENT MOTHS IN CARPETS.

ANY one of a benevolent disposition, who has ever on house-cleaning day observed the prudent housewife attentively examine the edges of carpets for moths, would surely wish that these little insects grew as large as bed bugs, so that such excessive straining of the eyes might be avoided.

When carpets are taken up, if there is any appearance of moths, sprinkle powdered Brimstone on the floor, befor the carpet is laid down again, and it is a good plan to let it remain after the carpet is tacked down. Tobacco and Black Pepper are also much used for this purpose, and will effectually guard against moths.

293.—TO PRESERVE CARPETS.

IT is very advisable in laying down carpets, to first cover the floor with large sheets of paper, which will prevent the dust from rising between the boards, and where the floor is uneven, it will prevent the carpet from being cut by the sharp edges of the flooring. By adopting this precaution a carpet will last much longer. Straw matting is better than straw to place underneath carpets, as the matting is smooth and even and the dust will not sift through it.

294.—TRANSPOSING THE BREADTHS.

THIS prudent plan of managing carpets is doubtless familiar to many ladies, but to others it may be a novelty. Certain portions of the carpet about the entry and around the hearth, which are the most used, always wear rapidly, while the back breadths that are little used, remain as bright and good as new. Before the most exposed parts are too badly worn, it is good policy to transpose the breadths and bring the unused portions into service. The whole carpet can be thus made to wear evenly and twice the usual service will be obtained.

295.—STAIR CARPETS.

STAIR carpets should always have a strip of paper placed underneath them. The strip should be placed just over the edges of each stair-step, as this is the place where the carpet generally first wears through. The friction of the carpet against the boards underneath will be thereby lessened. The strips should be about four or five inches in breadth, and within an inch or two as long as the carpet is wide. This plan will preserve a stair carpet in good condition a much longer time than it would otherwise keep. A strip of old carpet answers better than paper.

296.—SWEEPING CARPETS.

PERSONS who are accustomed to use refuse tea leaves while sweeping the carpet and find that they leave stains, will do well to employ fresh cut grass instead. It is better than tea leaves for preventing dust and gives the carpet a very bright fresh look. Moist

Bread is also good. In the room of the sick, strew fresh cut grass and flowers cut in pieces or pulled apart, over the carpet before sweeping. They will give a sweet pleasant fragrance, quite agreeable to the patient, and they will prevent the dust from rising.

297.—MANAGEMENT OF BROOMS.

BY bestowing a little extra care upon brooms, ladies can continually receive the benefit expressed in the familiar adage, "a new broom sweeps clean." On every washing day, immerse the brooms for a few minutes in boiling soap-suds, which process will render the broom-head pliantly tough, so that it will never cut the carpet. When brooms are not in use, ladies usually stand them against the wall, and the weight of the broom causes the broom straws to bend out of their proper shape. If they are always hung up by the handle, this trouble will be avoided. Managed in the above manner a broom will last much longer and always sweep like a new broom.

298.—FLOORS.

IN some countries it is not customary to cover the floors with carpet. Throughout all the Southern States, the absence of carpets is especially noticeable;

many a county in the South might be traversed and not a single carpet seen even among the wealthiest classes. The tidy housewives of those countries, however, are as particular about keeping the floor of the best room clean and spotless, as they would be about the choicest Brussels carpet. Nothing of course can excel a thorough scrubbing with soap and water to clean dirty floors, but there are many substances, however, like oil, grease and ink, which penetrate into the pores of the wood, and cannot be extracted with soap and water. To remove such stains a special treatment is required.

299.—OIL AND GREASE SPOTS.

TO remove oil or grease spots from floors, employ the following method. Take a quarter of a pound each of Fuller's Earth and Pearlash, and boil them in a quart of soft water, While the mixture is hot, lay some of it on the spots and allow it to remain about ten or twelve hours, at the expiration of which time, scour off the mixture with sand and water. If a floor is badly covered with grease spots, it should be washed over with this mixture the day before it is scoured. Fuller's Earth and Ox Gall boiled together, form a very powerful cleansing mixture for floors. Strong

Pearlash water mixed with sand, and rubbed on floors or tables stained with grease, is also considered one of the most effective means that can be used to extract grease.

300.—INK, PAINT, VARNISH, &C.

INK stains upon floors, and also stains produced by any liquid containing coloring matter, can always be removed as follows: When soap and water will not affect these stains, wash them thoroughly with very strong Vinegar or salts of Lemon. Paint, varnish, &c., can be removed from floors by Spirits of Turpentine or chloroform. The several classes of stains included in this method can be removed from carpets also by the use of the same agents.

301.—TO KEEP FLOORS OF A GOOD COLOR.

AN excellent way to scour floors and at the same time keep them of a good color, is the following: Mix together Lime one part; sand three parts, soft-soap two parts. Apply a little of this mixture to the floor with the scrubbing brush and rub thoroughly; then rinse with clean water and rub dry. This will also keep away all sort of vermin.

302.—MAHOGANY COLOR FOR FLOORS.

IT often happens that dining-room, kitchen, and other floors are exceedingly troublesome, consequent upon repeated spilling of grease, and upon continued care and worry on the part of the tidy housewife, in striving to guard against such accidents. The finest hotels and most aristocratic families have recently adopted an admirable plan of dressing floors, which give to them a rich brown or mahogany-like color, thus entirely doing away with spotting and scouring of grease spots. Take quarter of a pound of Burnt Umber to half gallon of Linseed Oil, and add a small quantity of Litharge, to act as a dryer. Mix the ingredients and heat to a boiling temperature, then while the preparation is hot, rub it into the floor with a flannel cloth. If preferred a small quantity of Spanish Brown may be added, which will give a still brighter hue. If a a fine finish is desired, the floor may be occasionally wiped with a waxed brush or cloth. The above quantity of the dressing will be ample for a room of moderate size. A floor thus dressed should never be scoured with soap, sand, or any other scouring preparation whatever. When it becomes soiled by the settling of dust, (which is likely to be till repeated washings), merely wash it with skim milk, butter-milk, or even dish water. This treatment of floors possesses several advantages: it is decidedly labor saving, as the floor never requires scouring—even if grease falls upon it there will be no spot; again, it is economical, for no soap need ever be applied. The prime object, however, is to give the floor the same elegant appearance and rich color possessed by old mahogany furniture. The dressing should be repeated at least once in twelve months.

303.—CLEANING STRAW MATTING.

STRAW matting may be readily cleaned and its color preserved by this treatment. Make a solution of Salt and soft water, using considerable salt, but have it completely dissolved. Rub the matting with a large coarse cloth, frequently dipping it in the solution; after which, the matting should be well wiped until dry. The use of the Salt will prevent straw matting from turning yellow.

304.—CARE OF OIL CLOTHS.

TO clean oil cloths and keep them looking fresh, wash them once a month with skim milk and water, in equal proportions; then every three months wash them in boiled Linseed Oil. Use very little oil, but rub it well in with a rag, and then polish with a piece of old silk. With this kind of treatment oil-cloths will last for years and always have a bright appearance. Never use a brush, or soap, or very hot water, as the paint will be thereby injured.

305.—OIL MARKS UPON WALL PAPER.

THOUGHTLESS persons are quite prone to tilt back a chair and rest their heads against the costly papered wall of the parlor or drawing room; and the invariable result is a conspicuous oil mark. Visitor's children too, delight to pass their greasy hands over satin wall paper, to see if it really is as soft as it looks, or they try to pick of the gilt flowers. The mistress of the house views the mischief with dismay, but politeness keeps her silent. These oil marks may be removed however, as follows: Mix to the consistency of cream finely ground Pipe Clay with water. Put a layer of the creamy mixture upon the spots and let it remain until dry. It will dry by the following day, when the powder may be easily removed with a penknife or brush. The drying may be hastened by covering the mixture with a sheet of paper, and then applying for a few seconds, an iron only moderately warm. On using

India Rubber to remove the dust taken up by the grease, the paper will be found restored to its original whiteness and opacity. This simple method has proved highly successful, and was remarkably so in an instance where the folio of a ledger had exhibited the marks of candle grease and snuff for more than twelve months.

CHAPTER XIV.

306.—RENOVATION OF BEDDING AND FEATHERS.

IT is a curious condition of our existence that about eight hours in every twenty-four, a third of a lifetime, must be passed in repose. Then too, the scenes, sights, and sensations of dreamland are pleasanter, and ofttimes far more thrilling or frightful than real ones. Nothing can excel a good bed for genuine luxury. What a sweet sense of comfort it imparts, when after the worry and labor of the day, its never failing aid is sought to invigorate the fatigued brain or muscles, and how reluctantly is the cosy nest among the soft feathers relinquished on cold mornings. Feather beds are heir-looms highly prized. Often they are transmitted from mother to daughter, and from grandam to posterity until they become nearly as cherished a family heritage as ancestral estates. Feather beds never wear out, but with age and use the ticking becomes soiled and the feathers heavy and matted together; yet by proper renovation from time to time they will afford many generations comfort.

A few methods are presented. No apology need be offered for their introduction in the Chemical Laundry Guide, for the value of such methods is shown by the premiums awarded them by societies devoted to the interests of science and art.

307.—RENEWAL OF FEATHER BEDS.

IN cities there are establishments where feather beds are perfectly renovated by steam, but the process employed would be impracticable for home use. By the accompanying simple treatment, however, feather beds that have become soiled and heavy can be readily rendered clean, sweet, and light. At first sight, the process may appear to be detrimental, yet it is not only an easy method, but attended with perfect success. Without emptying the beds, thoroughly scour the ticking with a clean stiff brush and strong hot soap-suds; then lay them on the roof of a shed or some other clean place where the rain will fall on them. In very dry weather, they may be made wet by several thorough sprinklings with a watering pot, but the wetting is much better effected by the rain. When thoroughly soaked, let them dry in the hot rays of the sun for six or seven consecutive days. Shake them up well and turn them over every day. If exposed to the night air they will become damp and then mildew, so they should be covered during the night, for the idea is, after they are once soaked through, to have them continue to dry without receiving additional moisture. This plan of washing the bed-ticking and feathers makes them very fresh and light. It is far easier than the usual mode of emptying the beds and washing the feathers separately, and it answers quite as well. Care must be taken to thoroughly air the bed before using it.

308.—CLEANSING FEATHERS.

THE following method of cleansing feathers of their animal oil gained a premium from the English Society of Arts. To every gallon of clean water that is used add a pound of Quicklime. Stir the Lime and water well together, and when the undissolved Lime precipitates in a fine powder, pour off the clear Lime water for use. Put the feathers to be cleansed into a tub, and pour over them a sufficient quantity of the solution to cover them about two inches, after they have been well stirred about therein, and allowed to settle. When thoroughly moistened, the feathers will sink to the bottom, and should be allowed to thus soak for three or four days; then lay them on a sieve to drain off all the foul liquor. The feathers should be afterwards washed in clean water and dried upon nets, the meshes of which may be about the fineness of cabbage nets. They should be shaken on the nets from time to time, and as they dry they will fall through the meshes and are to be collected for use. Plenty of air will be serviceable while they are drying. The process will be completed in about three weeks; and after being thus treated, the feathers will only need beating to free them from any dust which may have settled on them.

309.—HAIR MATTRESSES.

HAIR mattresses, even the most expensive ones, by use soon become hard and uneven, and are then anything but comfortable. The reason why they get in this condition in so short a time is, that at manufactories where hair mattresses are made, the hair was never properly picked free from bunches. The hair is usually stored away in large quantities, where it becomes matted together in knots and bunches. In this condition it is made into mattresses, and although at first the mattress seems smooth and even, as soon as it sustains a continued weight, as a person lying upon it, the bunches become apparent. If a mattress that has become hard and dirty be subjected to the accompanying treatment, it will be rendered a better mattress than when first bought. Simply rip the ticking apart and wash it; then carefully pick the hair free from bunches and let it remain in a dry airy place for several days. When the ticking is dry, fill it lightly with the hair and tack it together. The hair is not likely to again get in bunches.

310.—WASHING BED FURNITURE.

IN washing all sorts of heavy bed furniture it is a wise plan, before immersing the articles in water, to shake off or beat out as much of the dust as possible, as thereby the labor of cleansing will be greatly decreased. In the case of colors, and especially mixed colors, no Soda, Pearlash, or Washing Crystal should be used, as the colors might be injured. Mottled soap is the best to employ for these articles, and use plenty of soft water, not hot, but warm. On wringing out of the second washing water, dip each piece immediately into cold hard water for finishing. Shake them out well and let them dry as quickly as possible. If it be desirable to starch them, the starch may be stirred into the rinsing water.

311.—HEAVY COUNTERPANES AND QUILTS.

IN the case of very heavy cottons, counterpanes, quilts, &c., which to wash and wring in the usual way is very tiresome, a mode of scouring may be adopted with advantage. Cut into thin slices a pound of mottled soap and add a quarter of an ounce of Potash and an ounce of Pearlash; then pour a pailful of boiling water over the mixture, and let it stand until the ingredients completely dissolve. Now put into the scouring tub a pailful or more of warm water and a bowlful of the soap solution. Lay in the counterpane and pound it well with a clothes pounder, often turning the counterpane over in the tub. When this has been done, wring it across a hook or wooden peg, which manner of wringing is effected as follows. Swing the middle of the counterpane over the peg, turn the opposite ends of the article around each other, place a clean clothestick between them, and then wring by twisting around the stick. In this way the article may be wrung with ease and as dry as possible; the harder it is wrung without tearing it, the better. After this first scouring, pass the counterpane through a second liquor prepared like the first. Wring it out again and rinse in clear cold water. (The first and second liquors need not be wasted, but other cotton or woolen articles may be passed through them.) Now pour into the rinsing tub a sufficient quantity of boiling water and add a small quantity of the soap solution, just enough to produce a thin lather; then add about three tablespoonfuls of liquid blue, and the acid of the blue acting upon the alkali of the Pearlash and soap will cause a slight fermentation or effervescence. Stir this blue liquid with a stick and immerse the counterpane. Again use the pounder about five minutes and the counterpane will be colored a fine azure blue of light shade, but as it dries in the sun and wind the blue mostly disappears, leaving a brilliant white.

312.—BED COVERS IN RELIEVO OR EMBOSSED WORK.

BED furniture of embossed patterns, or ornamented with prominent flowered figures, or fashioned in relievo or raised work, require a special treatment in ironing, or else the embossed and relievo work will be all pressed together and the prominent portions apt to become glazed. In fact, they ought not to be submitted at all to the usual process of smoothing, but should be folded while quite damp as in (313), then laid between two clean boards or table leaves, a heavy weight placed above, and in this position allowed to dry. Treated in this way the embossed pattern will have a clear outline.

313.—IRONING AND FOLDING SHEETS, BED SPREADS, &C.

THE following method of folding sheets, counterpanes, and bed spreads allows the articles to be conveniently spread over the bed, and in the case of outside bed spreads, the creases made by the folds will disappear. It is the plan used by the soldiers of the French army for folding army blankets. It is unnecessary to iron but one side, and the proper side to iron is usually the right side, but sometimes when the counterpane is of a choice design of flowers or raised work, it is best to apply the iron to the wrong side. Begin by folding the article lengthwise with the surface that is to be ironed on the inside; then take the outer edges and bring them even with the middle crease, thus exposing for ironing half of the surface that was folded in, a breadth above and a breadth underneath. After both of these breadths are ironed, bring over the newly formed creases even with the middle crease, and two new breadths will be exposed for ironing, one above and the other underneath. After ironing these new breadths, reverse the middle crease, which will bring the last formed creases even, and when the unironed portion thus exposed above and underneath is smoothed, one surface of the article will be ironed and properly folded lengthwise. Now fold it crosswise and bring the outer ends even with the middle crease, and the ironing and folding of the bed spread will be completed.

314.—BED BUGS.

THE discussion of the renovation of beds and bedding cannot be more appropriately dismissed than by presenting a bed bug exterminator. History does not record the time when man was first annoyed by bed bugs; so their advent is a matter of speculation. They can hardly be of ancient origin, however, for they would surely have been included in the plagues that were sent to make the hard heart of Pharoah relent.

The presence of chinches is usually regarded as an index of filth and careless housekeeping, yet such is not always the case, however. In large cities especially, nearly every family is troubled with these little pests. The walls and floors of houses contain millions of them, and unless the greatest precaution is taken they will not remain there, but sally forth on nightly forages. Again, the former occupants of a house may have left them, and when discovered by the tidy housewife she has "conniptions." There may also be imported cases but it would hardly be convenient to place a quarantine upon visitors. By stringent measures, however, the enemy may be vanquished.

315.—TO DESTROY THEM WHEN IN THE WALLS AND FLOOR.

BED bugs may be totally annihilated when in the walls and floors by the fumes of burning Sulphur. Close tightly every crack, fire-place, window and door of the room, then for several hours let Brimstone burn on Charcoal in an iron kettle. Afterward thoroughly air the room. This plan will also effectually destroy cockroaches.

316.—TO KEEP THEM AWAY FROM THE BEDS.

THE most successful substance that can be employed for driving away chinches is Quicksilver. It cannot be applied by itself, but requires a vehicle or menstruum to convey it. It is frequently mixed with Lard, but the Whites of Eggs are much superior, for a mixture of Quicksilver and Eggs will not in the least injure the furniture. To the Whites of four or five Eggs add about a tablespoonful of Quicksilver, and cream the whole well together. Be sure to add the Quicksilver before beating the Eggs. Apply the mixture with a feather wherever they "most do congregate." Tansy strewn over the slats or sacking bottom of the bed is very effectual for driving them away. Filling the crevices of the bedstead with Putty, or if old, painting or varnishing it, will often keep them away.

317.—SPIRITS OF NAPHTHA.

SPIRITS of Naphtha rubbed with a small painter's brush into every part of the bedstead is a quite sure way of freeing it from bugs. The mattress and binding of the bed should be examined and the same process applied there, as they generally harbor more in these parts than in the bedstead. Five cents worth of Naphtha is sufficient for one bed.

318.—EXPLANATION OF INDEX.

THE General Index has been arranged with a view of making it of the most convenience possible for ready reference. It will be readily seen by glancing over its columns, that the promise of the Chemical Laundry Guide has been fulfilled:—that there is scarcely an article of any material that admits of washing or renovating, but what has been considered; that there is hardly a method or process employed by the professional Launderer that has not been presented. The numbers in the Index, as well as the numerals throughout the book, refer to the numbers of the methods, and not to the page numbers. The methods are arranged alphabetically; and when any reference is sought, refer to the noun representing the desired process, or to the name of the material under treatment, and not to qualifying words, for examples; if it be desirable to raise the plush of velvet, a suitable method is given under Velvets; if point lace is to be renovated, refer to Laces; if a wine stain is to be extracted, the process will be found in the column of Stains. The Index, however, is very complete and difficulty in finding any method will rarely happen. Each chapter too, prevents a distinct department of skillful laundry work. Whenever any delicate laundry experiment is proposed, or when a difficult laundry operation would be of advantage but is deemed perhaps impossible, it always will be profitable to refer to the Chemical Laundry Guide.

319.—GENERAL INDEX.

A

Advantages of Corrugated Glossing Iron............. 14
Alpacas—Oriental Method of Washing... 172
Alpacas—Treatment of....................................164
Aniline Blue.. 61
Antimacassars—Ironing....................................230
Applying Starch to Shirts................................... 8
Aromatic Herbs...128

B

Bedding—Renovation of....................................306
Bed Bugs...314
Bed Bugs—To destroy in Walls and Floors..........315
Bed Bugs—To keep away from Beds...................316
Bed Covers in Relievo or Embossed Work...........312
Bed Furniture—Washing...................................310
Beds—Renewal of Feathers...............................307
Bed Spreads—Folding and Ironing.....................313
Beetles—To keep away from Linen....................130

Benzoin—Caution in Using............................213
Benzoin Stains—To remove............................212
Black Reviver—For Silks and Leather................219
Blankets—Ironing Woolen.............................186
Bleach—For Brown Sheeting........................... 39
Bleach—For Faded Articles...........................174
"Bleach"—Laundry.................................... 39
Bleaching White Goods—German Method................. 40
Bleaching Wool......................................195
Bleaching Woolens and Flannels......................191
Blond Lace—To Revive................................233
Blond Lace—To Wash..................................232
Blue Aniline.. 61
Blue—Chinese Soluable............................... 62
Blueing Clothes..................................... 60
Bobbinets—Starch for................................ 28
Bombazet—Treatment of...............................171
Bombazine—Treatment of..............................164
Book Muslin—Washing.................................171
Broad Cloth—Cleaning................................277
Brocatello Tapestry.................................226
"Broke Water"—Method of Preparing................... 51
Brooms—Management of................................297

C

Calicos—Treatment of................................164
Cambrics—Treatment of...............................171

Cambrics—Washing—Oriental Method..............172
Care of Linen...127
Care of Linen—An Agreeable Perfume..............131
Care of Linen—Disinfecting.............................136
Care of Linen—Lavender Scent Bag..................129
Care of Linen—Laying away Summer Goods.........133
Care of Linen—Marking Articles......................134
Care of Linen—To keep away Moths, &c............130
Care of Oil Cloths..304
Care of Sad-Irons... 21
Care of Shirt Board...................................... 12
Carpets—Renovation of.................................285
Carpets—Borax 288
Carpets—Carpet Cleaners' Method....................283
Carpets—Carpets slightly Soiled......................291
Carpets—Grease spots..................................287
Carpets—Magnesia Paste 290
Carpets—Oil on Carpets................................289
Carpets—Stair..295
Carpets—Sweeping......................................296
Carpets—To Preserve...................................293
Carpets—To prevent Moths............................292
Carpets—Transposing the Breadths..................294
Chintzes—Treatment of.................................164
Chocolate Stains...100
Clay Stains—Red Shale and Clay....................121
Clothes—Assorting...................................... 59

Clothes Lines—To Preserve............................ 24
Clothes Pins—To Preserve............................ 24
Clothing—Gentlemen's......................................270
Clothing—Cleaning with Soap Bark...................279
Clothing—Cleaning Woolen..............................189
Clothing—Cleansing Broadcloth........................277
Clothing—Colored Pantaloons..........................278
Clothing—General Stain Method......................276
Clothing—Grease Spots...................................271
Clothing—Making Old Clothes New..................284
Clothing—Pearlash and Lime Liquid..................272
Clothing—Pressing Pants.................................283
Clothing—Springing Pants...............................282
Clothing—To Raise the Nap on Cloth................281
Clothing—To Remove Acid Stains....................273
Clothing—To Remove Alkaline Stains..............274
Clothing—To Remove Paint and Wax Stains........275
Clothing—To Render Water-Proof..................... 33
Clothing—To Renovate Rusty Black.................280
Coffee Stains..100
Collars—Construction of.................................163
Collars—Different Styles of.............................162
Collars—Molding or Twisting........................... 17
Collars—Raised Embroidery and Flowered.......... 42
Collars—Starching... 9
Colored Articles—Starch for............................. 29
Color of new goods rendered Permanent..............170

Colors—Oriental Method of Washing..................172
Colors—Printed Goods of Delicate....................164
Colors—To Set Various...............................167
Colors—Vegetable.................................... 58
Contents.. 4
Corrugated Glossing and Molding Iron................ 13
Corrugated Glossing Iron—Advantages of.............. 14
Corrugating Glossing Iron—Care of................... 20
Corrugated Glossing Iron—How to Operate............. 15
Cotton—Stains on.................................... 91
Counterpanes—Ironing and Folding....................313
Counterpanes—To Wash Heavy..........................311
Crape...228
Crape Scarf—To Wash a...............................246
Crape—To Restore Rusty Italian......................244
Crape—To Restore Stained Black......................243
Creamy Tint of Laces................................237
Crotchet—Ironing....................................230
"Crutching"—Toilet Soap............................. 85
Cuffs—Molding or shaping............................ 17
Cuffs—Starching..................................... 9

D

Damask Tapestry.....................................226
Disenfecting Apparel—Sure Method....................136

E

Elderly Gentlemen's Shirt—Cutting and Making...159
Embroidering New Linen.................................. 42
Embroidery—To Iron....................................... 42
Explanation of Index......................................318
Extra Fine Gloss.. 16

F

Family Right... 1
Feather Beds—Renewal of...............................307
Feathers—Cleansing.......................................308
Feathers—Renovation of.................................306
Filtering Water through Charcoal...................... 46
Filtering Water through Spongy Iron................. 47
Fire-Proof—To Render Garments......................137
Flannels..176
Flannels.—A Quick Method for Bleaching.........191
Flannels—Hot Suds for..................................183
Flannels—Ironing Red...................................185
Flannels—Shrinking......................................180
Flannels—To Produce a Beautiful White............190
Flannels—To Remove Grease from....................177
Flannels—To Restore the Glossy Finish of..........192
Flannels—To Wash Red..................................189
Flannels—Washing Choice..............................184
Floors...298

Floors—To Remove Ink, Paint, Varnish, &c.........300
Floors—Mahogany Color for...........................302
Floors—Oil and Grease Spots.........................299
Floors—To Keep of Good Color........................301
Flour Starch—To Make Good........................... 27
Folding Shirts—Laundry Style........................ 19
Folding Table Linen................................. 45
French Chalk.......................................198
French Scouring Drops..............................199
Fruit Stains on Linen and Cotton.................... 93
Furs—Management of.................................265
Furs—Sable, Chinchilla, Squirrel, and Fitch........266
Furs—Stretching....................................268
Furs—To Keep away Moths............................269
Furs—White, Ermine, Minever, &c....................267

G

Gauze—To Gloss and Finish..........................249
General Index......................................319
Gentlemen's Clothing...............................270
Ginghams— Oriental Method of Washing...............172
Ginghams—Treatment of..............................164
Gloss—Extra Fine................................... 16
Glossing Iron—Corrugated Glossing and Molding... 13
Glossing Iron. How to Operate...................... 15
Glossing Linen..................................... 6
Glossy Finish of Woolens and Flannels..............192

Glue Starch... 30
Grease Spots...122
Grease Spots of Long Standing.....................178
Grease—To Preserve..................................... 67
Gui Pure D'Art—Lace—Ironing.....................230
Gum Arabic Starch...................................... 28

H

Handkerchiefs—Folding and Ironing................. 45
Handkerchiefs—Wrinkles in Silk....................251
Hats, Felt—To Renovate with Soap Bark...........279
Holders for Sad-Irons................................... 23
Honey Mixture..221
Hose—Lamb's Wool.....................................194
Hose—To Whiten Flannel or Woolen...............193
Hose—Washing Silk....................................224

I

Indelible Ink..134
Indelible Ink—Formula for Making.................135
Ink Spots—To Remove.................................102
Introduction to Fine Laundry Work.................. 5
Iron and Starch White Vests.......................... 41
Ironing and Folding Table Linen..................... 45
Iron Rust—To Remove.................................101
Isinglass Starch.. 31

J

Javelle Water... 57

K

Kid Gloves...257
Kid Gloves—French..260
Kid Gloves—Ganleine..263
Kid Gloves—Opera Kids of Light Shade.....................262
Kid Gloves—Perfume for.......................................132
Kid Gloves—Perfume for.......................................264
Kid Gloves—Stains on..258
Kid Gloves—To Clean without Wetting.....................261
Kid Gloves—Washing..259

L

Laces..228
Laces—Creamy Tint..237
Laces—Curtains Laundrying.................................... 43
Laces—Curtains Laying Away................................133
Laces—Fine Thread..234
Laces—Ironing..230
Laces—Ironing Fine...231
Laces—Magnesia and French Chalk for....................238
Laces—Parisian Method of Washing Point.................235
Laces—Perfume for Delicate..................................132
Laces—Reviving Blond...233

Laces—Silver and Gold..................................240
Laces—Sugar Sizing for...............................236
Laces—To Clear Starch................................229
Laces—To Wash Black..................................239
Laces—To Wash White Silk or Blond...............232
Lace Veil—To Wash a Black...........................242
Lace Veil—To Wash a White...........................241
Lamas—Treatment of....................................164
Lamas—Washing..171
Lamas—Washing—Oriental Method..................172
Laundry "Bleach"... 38
Lavender Scent Bag......................................129
Lawns—Starch for... 28
Lawns—Treatment of....................................164
Lawns—Washing..171
Lawns—Washing—Oriental Method..................172
Leather—Black Reviver for...........................220
Lemon—Essential Salts.................................104
Linens—Care of...127
Linens—Glossing... 6
Linens—Laying Away for Summer..................133
Linens—Marking...134
Linens—Stains on... 91
Linens—Suits, Color and Lustre..................... 44
Linens—To Restore Scorched........................126
Linens—To Whiten Yellow............................. 37
Lye—To Make Good...................................... 66

M

Mahogany Color for Floors....................302
Matting—To Clean Straw......................303
Mattresses—Hair.............................309
Merinoes—Treatment of.......................164
Merinoes—Washing............................171
Merinoes—Washing Oriental Method............172
Mildew—To Extract...........................107
Milk Stains.................................114
Modern Shirt Cutting and Making.............144
Molding Collars and Cuffs.................... 17
Molder—How to Operate........................ 18
Molding Iron................................. 13
Moths from Carpets..........................292
Moths from Clothes..........................130
Moths from Furs.............................269
Mourning Dresses............................243
Mousse de Laines—Treatment of...............164
Mousse de Laines—Washing....................171
Mousse de Laines—Washing—Oriental Method....172
Muslins—Congree Starch for................... 34
Muslins—To Shrink...........................140
Muslins—To Starch............................ 35
Muslins—To Thicken and Strengthen............ 36

N

Napkins—Ironing and Folding.......................... 45
Napkins—Stained.................................... 99
Napkins—Stains on White...........................123
Napkins—Vegetable Stains........................... 92
Naphtha for Bed Bugs...............................317
Nap—To Raise on Cloth..............................281
Nap—To Raise on Velvet.............................255

O

Oil Cloths—Care of.................................304
Oil Marks upon Wall Paper..........................305
Ox Gall—To Preserve................................168
Ox Gall Soap....................................... 83

P

Paint—To Extract from Any Material................210
Pants—Pressing....................................283
Pants—Springing...................................282
Patterns—Cutting Shirt............................138
Percales—Treatment of.............................171
Percales—French Method of Washing.................173
Percales—Oriental Method of Washing...............172
Perfume for Clothes...............................131
Perfume for Kid Gloves............................132

Perfume for Kid Gloves.................................264
Piques—Treatment of......................................171
Piques—French Method of Washing..................173
Piques—Oriental Method of Washing...............172
Piques—To Starch... 35
Plaid Shawls—To Wash—Scotch Method..........187
Plush on Velvet—To Raise...............................255
Potato Liquor...218
Potato Starch... 26
Preface.. 3
Preparing Starch—Laundry Method.................. 7
Printed Goods of Delicate Colors.....................164
Printed Goods—Washing. Oriental Method.......172
Printed Table Covers......................................175
Prints—Agents for Special Colors.....................169
Prints—General Hints for Ironing....................166
Prints—General Hints for Washing..................165
Prints—French Method of Washing..................173
Prints—Oriental Method of Washing Bright......172
Prints—To Bleach Faded Articles....................174
Prints—To Render Colors Permanent...............170
Prints—To Set Various Colors.........................167
Prints—Washing Goods of Delicate Colors.........171
Purchasing Contract...................................... 2

Q

Quick Method of Bleaching Flannel..................191

Quilts—To Wash and Wring Heavy..................311

R

Ribbons...228
Ribbons...247
Ribbons Creased....................................250
Ribbons—Isinglass Sizing for..................249
Ribbons—Perfume for.............................132
Ribbons Soiled......................................248
Ribbons—To Stiffen...............................252
Ribbons—Wrapping................................253
Rose Pink... 63
"Rough Dry"—Laying Away Summer Goods......133
Rust Eaten Sad-Irons............................ 22

S

Sad-Irons—Care of................................ 20
Sad-Irons—Encrusted with Oxide.............. 22
Sad-Irons—Holders................................ 23
Sad-Irons—Scouring............................... 21
Satins...228
Satins—Colored or White—To Wash..........217
Satins—Detergent Fluid.........................202
Satins—Treatment of.............................247
Satins—To Clean White and Flowered......256
Satins—To Extract Grease from...............254

Scarf—To Wash a China Crape..........................246
Scarf—Wrinkles in Silk....................................251
Shawls, Plaid—Scotch Method of Washing..........187
Shawls—Washing Silk......................................225
Sheeting—To Bleach... 39
Shirt Board—Self-Adjusting............................. 10
Shirt Board—Care of....................................... 12
Shirt Board—How to Use................................. 11
Shirts—Improved Method of Cutting and Making...138
Shirts—Selection of Material for......................139
Shirts—Shrinking the Muslin......,....................140
Shirts—Common Faults in the Fit of.................141
Shirts—Seven Measurements............................142
Shirts—Dimensions of Medium Sized..................143
Shirts—Modern.—Front Breadth......................144
Shirts—Shoulder Measurement..........................145
Shirts—The Shield Bosom................................146
Shirts—Back Breadth......................................147
Shirts—The Yoke..148
Shirts—Joining the Breadths.,.........................149
Shirts—Neck Band..150
Shirts—Sleeves...151
Shirts—Cuffs..152
Shirts—Inserting the Sleeves............................153
Shirts—Opening in Front.................................154
Shirts—Working...155
Shirts, Working—Back Breadth........................156

Shirts—The Yoke of Working..........................157
Shirts—Joining the Breadths of Working...........158
Shirts—Elderly Gentlemen's.............................159
Shirts—The Bosom..160
Shirts—To Strengthen the Bosom....................161
Shirts—Collars..162
Shirts—Construction of Collars 163
Shirts—A Pleasure to Iron............................. 10
Shirts—Laundry Style of Folding..................... 19
Silks—Renovation of....................................196
Silks—Acid Stains on Violet..........................205
Silks—Aqua Ammonia for.............................203
Silks—Benzoin Stains on..............................212
Silks—Black Reviver for...............................219
Silks—Chloroform for...................................204
Silks—Detergent Fluid for.............................202
Silks—Egg Method for Cleaning....................201
Silks—French Chalk....................................198
Silks—French Scouring Drops.......................199
Silks—Honey Mixture for Cleansing...............221
Silks—How to Use the Black Reviver.............220
Silks Lightly Soiled......................................223
Silks—Old Pitch, Varnish, or Oil Stains.........211
Silks—Ox Gall for..206
Silks—Potato Liquor for................................218
Silks—Preserving the Colors of......................216
Silks—Requisite Conditions in Renovating..........215

Silks—Spermaceti, Olein, and Sterin Stains on	208
Silks—To Remove Grease from	197
Silks—To Remove Grease from	200
Silks—To Remove Paint from	210
Silks—To Remove Resin Spots from	209
Silks—To Remove Wax Stains from	207
Silks—To Renovate with old Kid Gloves	222
Silks—To Wash	214
Silks—Washing	217
Silks—Washing Silk Shaws	225
Silks—Washing Silk Stockings	224
Silks—Washing Silk Tapestry	226
Silks—Worsted and Silk Reps	227
Soap Bark for Cleansing Purposes	279
Soaps of Domestic Manufacture	64
Soaps—Making Soft	65
Soaps—To Make Good Lye for	66
Soaps—To Preserve Grease for	67
Soaps—To Prevent Fatty Substances from Turning Rancid	68
Soaps—To Make Soft-Soap with Potash	69
Soaps—To Make Lye Soft	70
Soaps—Concentrated Lye for	71
Soaps—Labor Saving	72
Soaps—Turpentine	73
Soaps—To Convert Soft-Soaps into Hard	74
Soaps—Hard	75

Soaps—Home-Made Caustic Soda	76
Soaps—Domestic Hard	77
Soaps—Concentrated Lye Hard	78
Soaps—Hard White Tallow	78
Soaps—Cheap Family	80
Soaps—Myrtle	81
Soaps—Chemical	82
Soaps—Ox Gall	83
Soaps—Toilet	84
Soaps—"Crutching"	85
Soaps—Honey	86
Soaps—Mush	87
Soaps—Celebrated Windsor	88
Soaps—Glycerine	89
Soaps—Italian Honey	90
Springing Pants	282
Stains on White Linens and Cottons	91
Stains—Acid and Alkali	112
Stains—Acid and Tea	97
Stains—Aniline Red Magenta	118
Stains—Blood Stains of Long Standing	116
Stains—Claret and Port Wine	96
Stains—Clay and Shale	121
Stains—Essential Salts of Lemon for	104
Stains—Fruit	93
Stains—Fruit and Old Wine Stains	98
Stains—Grease Spots	122

Stains—Ink Spots..102
Stains—Ink or Iron Rust on Delicate Fabrics.......103
Stains—Iodine...117
Stains—Iron Rust...101
Stains—Iron Rust and Old Ink Spots....................105
Stains—Iron Rust—Sulphide of Ammonia............106
Stains—Method for Summer Use.........................111
Stains—Mildew...107
Stains—Mildew—Starch and Salt........................108
Stains—Mildew—Chloride of Lime.......................109
Stains—Mildew—Oxalic Acid...............................110
Stains—Milk..114
Stains—Nitric Acid..113
Stains—Non-Metallic...123
Stains on Napkins and Table Cloths.................... 99
Stains—Perspiration..115
Stains—Process of Sulphuration..........................100
Stains—Scorched Linen.......................................126
Stains—Scouring Balls for General Use..............124
Stains—Soot..119
Stains—Special Agents for Obstinate Cases......... 95
Stains—Stain Mixtures..125
Stains—Tar, Pitch, Resin, Paint, &c....................120
Stains—Vegetable Juices..................................... 92
Stains—Wine Stains in Linen.............................. 94
Starch—Applying to Shirts.................................. 8
Starches and Their Use....................................... 25

Starch—Congree for Muslins	34
Starch for Colored Articles	29
Starch—Gum Arabic	28
Starch—Glue	30
Starch—Isinglass	31
Starch—Laundry Method of Preparing	7
Starch—Potato	26
Starch—To Make Good Flour	27
Starch—To Starch Collars and Cuffs	9
Starch—Water-Proof	32
Sulphuration—Process of	100

T

Table Cloths Stained	99
Table Cloths—Stains on	123
Table Covers—Choice	175
Table Linen—Ironing and Folding	45
Tapestry—Damask and Brocatello	226
Toilet Soaps	84
Trimmings	228
Trimmings—To Stiffen Silk	252
Tub—Washing Wool	195

V

Veils—To Wash a Black Lace	242
Veils—To Wash a White Lace	241

Velveteens..255
Velvets...228
Velvets—Chloroform for..................................204
Velvets—Detergent Fluid for...........................202
Velvets—Grease on...199
Velvets—The Treatment of...............................247
Velvets—To Extract Grease from.....................254
Velvets—To Raise the Pile on...........................255
Vests—To Starch and Iron White...................... 41

W

Wall Paper—Oil Marks upon............................305
Washing... 46
Washing Compound—French............................ 56
Washing Compound—Javelle Water................. 57
Washing Crystals... 52
Washing Crystals—Borax.................................. 55
Washing Crystals—Detergent Fluid.................. 54
Washing Crystals—English Method.................. 53
Water Hard.. 50
Water Hard—Method of Preparing "Broke Water". 51
Water Turbid—Popular Methods of Clearing....... 48
Water Turbid—To Clear with Eggs and Vinegar... 49
Water-Proof—New Process of Rendering Cloth..... 33
Water-Proof Starch... 32
Water Stains on Black Crape............................245
Wine Stains... 94

Woolen Clothes—To Clean................................188
Woolen Shawls—Scotch Method of Washing........187
Woolens..176
Woolens—Black Stains on Scarlet.......................179
Woolens—Colored..182
Woolen—Spirits of Ammonia for........................178
Woolens—To Remove Grease from.....................177
Woolens—Washing Choice..................................184
Woolens—White...181
Wool—Tub Washing and Bleaching....................195
Working Shirt—Cutting and Making...................155
Worsted Reps...227
Worsted—Table Covers......................................175
Wrapping Ribbons..250
Wrapping—White Satins.....................................253

Y

Yellow Clay Stains..121
Yellow Sulphide of Ammonia..............................106
Yellow Linens—To Bleach.................................. 37

www.ingramcontent.com/pod-product-compliance
Lightning Source LLC
Chambersburg PA
CBHW031946230426
43672CB00010B/2064